BEASTLY BRAINS

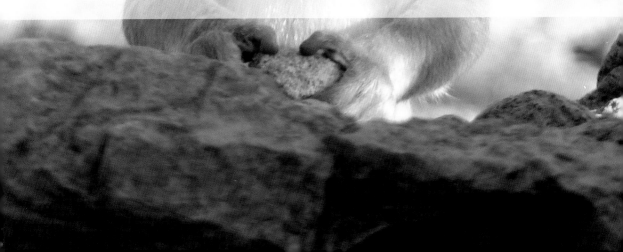

BEASTLY BRAINS

EXPLORING HOW ANIMALS
TALK, THINK, AND FEEL

NANCY F. CASTALDO

ghton Mifflin Harcourt
Boston New York

For my mom, who taught me that animals have brains when I was just learning that I had one myself. —N.F.C.

www.hmhco.com

The text type was set in Albertina MT and Zemestro.
The display type was set in Trend.

Library of Congress Cataloging-in-Publication Data

Names: Castaldo, Nancy F. (Nancy Fusco), 1962– author.
Title: Beastly brains : exploring how animals talk, think, and feel / Nancy F. Castaldo.
Description: Boston ; New York : Houghton Mifflin Harcourt, 2017. | "2016 |
    Audience: Ages 12+– | Audience: Grades 7 to 8.–
Identifiers: LCCN 2015045421 | ISBN 9780544633353
Subjects: LCSH: Animal intelligence—Juvenile literature. | Cognition in
    animals—Juvenile literature. | Animal behavior—Juvenile literature.
Classification: LCC QL785 .C3155 2017 | DDC 591.5/13—dc23 LC record available at
http://lccn.loc.gov/2015045421

Manufactured in China
SCP 10 9 8 7 6 5 4 3 2 1
4500615554

CONTENTS

Clearly, animals know more than we think, and think a great deal more than we know.

—Irene M. Pepperberg

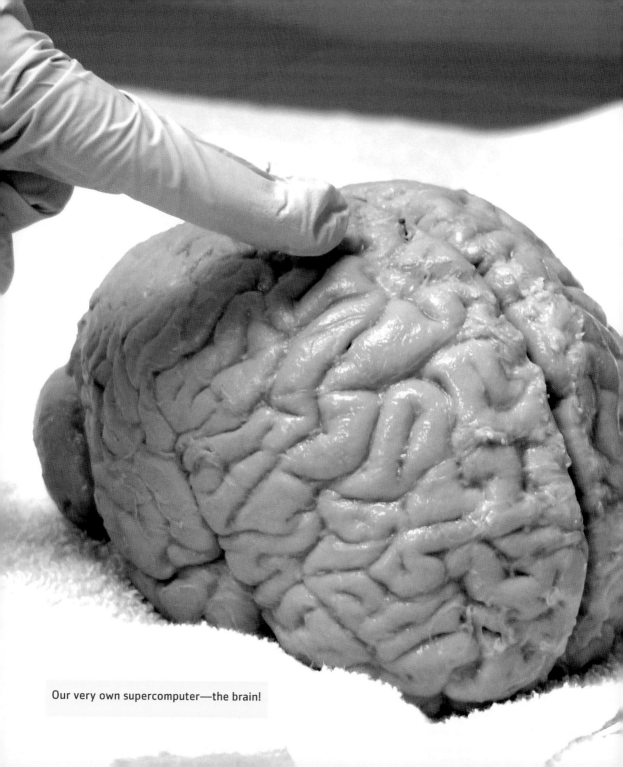

Our very own supercomputer—the brain!

OUR AMAZING BRAIN

e are *human!*

r own mini supercomputers in our heads. Our brains
unds (1.2 kilograms) and house all the information
he organ is the center of our intelligence, the initiator
ts, and the source of our behavior.

nly ones in the animal kingdom to have such a re-
odies. Brains come in all shapes and sizes; the larg-
whale (17.5 pounds/7 kilograms) and the tiniest to
004 pounds/2 grams).

oesn't necessarily indicate the intelligence of an ani-
relation to its body's dimensions that points to brain-
ured in the form of the encephalization quotient, or
EQ. Humans don't have the
largest brain, but they do
have the largest brain in relation to their body size, or

This display depicts the relative sizes of brains, the largest being the fin whale, and the human brain between the elephant's and the orangutan's.

1

The EQ of a human is 7. Dolphins have an EQ of 4.2, closer to ours than any other animal's.

EQ. An adult brain is generally about 2 percent of body weight with an EQ of 7. After us, the largest brain relative to body size is found in dolphins. In addition, the greater the number of folds in the cerebral cortex, the more intelligent the animal. It is believed that these folds provide more room for neurons. Dolphins are the only animal found to have more folds in their cortex than man.

According to Dr. Julie Pilitsis, an Albany Medical Center faculty physician in the Division of Neurosurgery, our brains are even larger in relation to our bodies when we are children, although they aren't yet fully developed. Experts suggest that our human brain doesn't fully mature until we are in our mid-twenties. All of the experiences you have and the behaviors you encounter up to that age may impact the formation of your brain.

Dr. Pilitsis points to the different sections of the preserved human brain resting in front of her on the table. "We're born with this blob of a brain and then it further develops," she says. She compares it to a house. "We are born with the basic architecture, but the other aspects you fill it with make it a house. It's the same with your brain."

We know a great deal about the human brain, but that knowledge is just a fraction of what there is to learn. For example, we know that the front part of our brain helps us make decisions, but we don't understand all the circuitry involved. Scientists and medical doctors, such as Dr. Pilitsis, are working every day to discover more and more about what makes us tick.

But this isn't a story about our human brains; it's about the brains of our fellow animals, and how they think and feel.

"Animals have those same support beams like we have in our brain, but different walls and furnishings," Dr. Pilitsis says, comparing our human brains to those of other animals.

As scientists work to uncover more about the brains of animals, they also find out additional information about human beings. Learning about how animals think and feel might make us look at them a bit differently. Are you up for the challenge?

FROM MACHINE TO THINKING ANIMAL

HOW SMART ARE ANIMALS?

You know your dog is smart. He might be able to ring a bell on a door to let you know he wants to go out, or he can find that tennis ball you threw to him last summer. He might even recognize some of the names of his toys. But did you ever wonder . . . just how smart is he? And how smart are other animals? It's possible that animals understand and feel emotion more than we think they do.

There are many questions about animal intelligence. Do animals share? How do they communicate with each other? What do they see when they look into a mirror? These are just a few. Questions are the starting blocks in the race of science.

Through research we know that monkeys steal. Crows recognize faces and use tools. Dolphins have a complex vocabulary. Rats demonstrate compassion. Dogs feel jealousy. And a hive full of honeybees makes decisions the same way we do via the neurons in our brain.

But those discoveries are recent. It might be hard to believe, but it wasn't long ago that animals were thought to be similar to machines—beings without thoughts or feelings, like the engine in a car.

What is this gorilla thinking as he sits against this wall?

A few scientists, such as Charles Darwin, thought otherwise and moved our thinking forward.

DARWIN'S BRAINY EARTHWORMS

Charles Darwin sat with his son, Francis, in a field outside his country home near London. The two were studying earthworms in the dim evening light.

Darwin was convinced the worms were turning over the soil, chewing it up and pooping it out. He believed this behavior was making the soil more fertile.

As he watched the worms drag leafy matter to plug up the holes to their burrows, he observed that sometimes worms dragged material by the tips of their bodies and sometimes by their middle section. Even in the low light Darwin could see that the segmented worms handled the leaves and needles differently at times.

He concluded that instinct or natural impulse led the worms to seal their burrows, but something else entirely was motivating the way they moved the material. If it wasn't instinct, what was it?

Worms have muscles beneath their skin that help them move. They also have tiny bristles called setae that help them grip the soil as they travel. Each of their segments has four pairs of setae.

"If we consider these several cases, we can hardly escape the conclusion that worms show some degree of intelligence in their manner of plugging up their burrows," wrote Darwin in *The Formation of Vegetable Mould Through the Action of Worms with Observations of Their Habits*, published in 1881.

Darwin's early work studying earthworms changed much of how we look at animals.

Darwin wasn't only making heads turn at this point in history with his theory of the origin of the species; now he was claiming that a lowly earthworm was exhibiting a form of intelligence? How ridiculous!

The scientific community dismissed the belief that animals could have any sort of cognition or understanding until Darwin published his studies. Centuries earlier the philosopher Aristotle had come up with a ladder-like thought system called *scala naturae* to rank creatures from low to high, with humans up there on the top rung, above all other mammals. Even though both Aristotle and Plato made remarks on the souls of animals, their intelligence had been overlooked.

PUNCH'S FANCY PORTRAITS.—No. 54

CHARLES ROBERT DARWIN, LL.D., F.R.S.

IN HIS *DESCENT OF MAN* HE BROUGHT HIS OWN SPECIES DOWN AS LOW AS POSSIBLE—*I.E.*, TO "A HAIRY QUADRUPED FURNISHED WITH A TAIL AND POINTED EARS, AND PROBABLY *ARBOREAL* IN ITS HABITS"—WHICH IS A REASON FOR THE VERY GENERAL INTEREST IN A "FAMILY TREE." HE HAS LATELY BEEN TURNING HIS ATTENTION TO THE "POLITIC WORM."

Darwin's *The Formation of Vegetable Mould Through the Action of Worms*, published in 1881, became very popular. It also drew criticism, as seen in this cartoon published in *Punch*.

In the seventeenth century the philosopher René Descartes dismissed all possibility of animals having any intelligence with two arguments: one against animals having thoughts, and the other against animals having reason. Descartes believed that humans' use of language is what sets us apart from animals. He believed that the ability of animals to convey anger, hunger, or fear through vocalizations was not the equivalent of the true language of humans. He believed that animals did not have souls and therefore did not also have minds. Animals were, therefore, nonthinking machines. His ideas were challenged by both Voltaire and Darwin.

Voltaire wrote in 1764:

What! that bird which makes its nest in a semi-circle when it is attaching it to a wall, which builds it in a quarter circle when it is in an angle, and in a circle upon a tree; that bird acts always in the same way? That hunting-dog which you have disciplined for three months, does it not know more at the end of this time than it knew before your lessons? Does the canary to which you teach a tune repeat it at once? Do you not spend a considerable time in teaching it? Have you not seen that it has made a mistake and that it corrects itself?

Voltaire believed that Descartes' views were wrong and that animals learn, solve problems, and correct themselves, therefore demonstrating that they do indeed have a mind.

Darwin believed that humans have continuously been physically evolving. This was not a popular view. Today scientists have taken this theory even further by suggesting that there is an evolution of cognition, meaning our minds have also evolved. The scientific community has been much slower to embrace this concept.

Even before he published his findings, Darwin wrote in a letter to his colleague George Romanes in 1881, saying, "It seems to me that they [worms] must be said to work with some intelligence, anyhow they are not guided by blind instinct."

Scientists have always had different approaches in their study of animal behavior. While Darwin confidently used firsthand observations, Romanes relied on the accounts of others' observations. Many considered these accounts to be mere anecdotes or stories and not part of the scientific method. Darwin was unique not only in his theories, but in how he developed them.

Skinner was known for his experiments involving a rat in a box. The rat would get a food reward when it got near a lever on the side of the box, then touched the lever, pushed the lever, and, finally, pushed the lever with its right paw. This learning process is known as *operant learning*, or *conditioning*. It involves shaping behavior rather than merely observing it. It's just like teaching your dog to sit by giving it a treat every time it follows your *sit* command.

This was a bold but calculated conclusion.

Darwin went on to claim that "various emotions and faculties, such as love, memory, attention, curiosity, imitation, reason, etc." might even be found in lower animals. Both the scientific community and the religious community were riled by these ideas. It's no wonder they were put aside for decades. Meanwhile, behaviorists continued to study white rats in laboratories, where scientists such as the American psychologist B. F. Skinner believed in and furthered Descartes' notion. They held on to the belief that all animal actions could be attributed to innate behavior or instinct. This led to the theory of behaviorism, in which animal behavior is explained by conditioning or training, with no consideration of thoughts or feelings.

MACHINES OR ROBOTS?

How did we finally move away from this belief? Well, not all scientists agreed with Descartes' ideas. The biologist Jakob Johann Baron von Uexküll was one of the first to challenge them.

In 1934 he wrote in *A Stroll Through the Worlds of Animals and Men:* "Many a zoologist and physiologist, clinging to the doctrine that all living beings are mere machines, denies their existence and thus boards up the gates to other worlds so that no single ray of light shines forth from all the radiance that is shed over them. But let us who are not committed to the machine theory consider the nature of machines." Von Uexküll continued, "We no longer regard animals as mere machines, but as subjects whose essential activity consists of perceiving and acting."

Much more recently, the ecologist Carl Safina wrote in *Orion Magazine* about the beliefs that were still pervasive in the seventies and eighties: "Wondering what feelings or thoughts might motivate behavioral [animal] acts became totally taboo. Radio blackout. Professional behaviorists could describe what they saw, period. Description—and only description—became 'the' science of animal behavior."

It took years to shed these old beliefs; for some, they still exist.

Konrad Lorenz, Niko Tinbergen, and Karl von Frisch made their marks as the founders of the new science of *ethology,* earning the Nobel Prize in 1973 "for their discoveries concerning organization and elicitation of individual and social behavior patterns."

It was no wonder these three had such a huge impact on the study of animals. All three men spent their childhoods among wild things. It was the larvae of a spotted salamander that young Lorenz reared to adulthood that sparked his curiosity. And it was a story by Selma Lagerlof that made him

There were two approaches to how scientists studied the way animals behaved. One branch, the early *ethologists* in Europe, studied instinct. They drew the conclusion that animals behaved a certain way because these behaviors were inborn. Early *behaviorists* in the United States studied learning. They believed that behavior was caused by external events and stimuli.

want to be a wild goose and then decide to raise domestic ducks. Lorenz became known for his imprinting studies with his ducklings.

As a child, Tinbergen spent hours watching the sticklebacks (spiny-backed fish) build nests in his backyard aquariums; later, in high school, he was put in charge of three saltwater aquariums. He was a natural observer, and an avid birdwatcher and camper. Tinbergen later studied instinctive behavior and became known for his behavioral experiments.

Von Frisch's uncle, who was an expert in insect vision, encouraged his nephew's early interest in animals. As an adult, von Frisch pioneered research on the communication of bees. All three men launched a science that has grown by leaps and bounds.

Another pioneer of ethology, Dame Jane Goodall, began to study and live with the chimpanzees at Gombe Stream National Park in Tanzania in 1960. Her studies showed the world that these animals had interpersonal relationships and an emotional intelligence. "You cannot share your life with any animal with a well-developed brain and not realize that animals have personalities," Goodall claims.

Jane Goodall first traveled to what is now Tanzania in 1960 when she was twenty-six years old to study the chimpanzees.

Being a bird brain might not be a bad thing. Alex, a gray parrot, could count to six and identify colors, and he formed a long relationship with the researcher Irene Pepperberg.

We can also thank the animal cognition scientist Irene Pepperberg and her African gray parrot, Alex, for another big leap forward. In 1977, she bought a parrot and began teaching him to speak. Pepperberg hoped that her parrot would one day be able to tell her how he saw the world and not just mimic her words.

Alex, with a brain the size of a walnut, was part of an interspecies study that lasted more than thirty years. During this time Pepperberg found that Alex understood concepts that were generally understood only by higher mammals, like primates. For example, the parrot knew the concepts of "same" and "different." Alex was also the first bird to learn the categories of shape and color. That showed an understanding of abstract categories. Unlike concrete categories, abstract categories can change to classify different things. For example, a red triangle could be grouped by color or shape.

Pepperberg's studies demonstrated that we are not alone in the ability to invent, deceive, plan, or think about ourselves. And further studies support this finding. It's amazing that we could ever have believed that animals are just machines.

Many researchers, like Dr. Brian Hare, who founded the dog intelligence assessment called Dognition, now recognize that intelligence is multifaceted. It's not an either/or situation. There are many types of intelligence.

Of course, how we see animals and recognize their intellect affects how we treat them. The strides made by scientists in the field of animal cognition directly impact the care of our pets, zoo animals, circus animals, and even the animals we breed for food.

⚡

Just examine the controversy about keeping intelligent creatures in captivity that was brought about by the 2013 documentary *Blackfish,* which focused on the treatment of orca whales, specifically one named Tilikum, in captivity. Tilikum was captured from the wild in 1983 and since 1991 has been held by SeaWorld in Orlando, Florida. Reports in the documentary suggest that stress in captivity led to the animal's aggressive behavior toward its trainers. "When you look into their eyes you know somebody is home," John Jett, a trainer, says about Tilikum in the movie. Although SeaWorld responded to the film with remarks about its commitment to the safety of its employees and guests and to the welfare of its animals, viewers spread their anger regarding the accusations online and through boycotts. The negative publicity eventually led SeaWorld to make changes to their orca shows, and they are beginning to phase them out altogether. But would *Blackfish* have provoked the same reaction if it had been filmed twenty years earlier? Probably not. Animal cognition research has provided a foundation, with *Blackfish* serving as a tipping point.

In 2016, Ringling Bros. and Barnum & Bailey Circus made a major change. They retired their Asian elephant act, which had frequently drawn criticism from animal rights activists. But why, after almost 150 years, did they

Elephants are highly emotional animals and very protective of their young. Circus treatment leads elephants to become unhealthy, depressed, and aggressive.

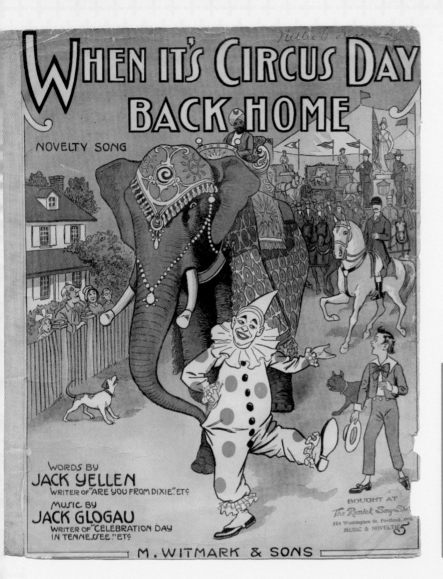

A century before we became fascinated with a grumpy cat on the Internet, there was a celebrity African elephant named Jumbo who gained worldwide attention first at the London Zoo and then with the Barnum & Bailey circus.

decide to remove the thirteen elephants from the center ring? According to the CEO of the Humane Society of the United States, the circus's decision to move its elephants to the Center for Elephant Conservation was, in the world of animal rights, comparable to how the fall of the Berlin Wall changed the view of Europe.

Sometimes your subject would rather study you than be studied.

Elephants are thinking animals with emotions, and they live with their families just like humans do. Imagine being pulled away from your mother and having her watch as you are put in chains, prodded, and beaten with batons. That's what circus elephants have to endure for years as performers in captivity. The more we learn about their emotional lives, the more we realize the need to protect them.

LOOKING AHEAD

Researchers have spent years analyzing the minds of animals, but today's science is revolutionizing past theories. Scientists are exploring the amazing problem-solving abilities of animals, studying their power to communicate, and even investigating their emotions to see if they exhibit any of the human complexities of mind.

ENTERING THE LAB
CLEVER HANS

It's 1891 and a crowd has gathered in a small town in Germany to see a horse solve math problems. That sounds crazy, right? Wilhelm von Osten, a German mathematics teacher, has taught his horse, Hans, to use his hoof to tap out the answers to math problems on a blackboard. No wonder people flock to see it; it's not every day you see a horse solving math.

Hans performs well. He gets a few wrong, but he impresses the crowd with his accuracy. He can even spell out names with his taps. Despite his achievements, there are critics in the crowd.

UNDER FIRE

Everyone thought Clever Hans was as smart as a thirteen- or fourteen-year-old human. Many thought that he could even tell time. But still others doubted his abilities. Experts were called in to determine if Clever Hans's answers were some sort of trick or if he truly was the smartest horse on earth. Could any horse be *that* smart?

After many examinations, Hans was found to be intelligent, but not the way everyone thought. The horse was actually responding to the slight, involuntary movements of his examiners. He may not have been able to solve the math problems, but Hans had sharp eyes for body language and was able

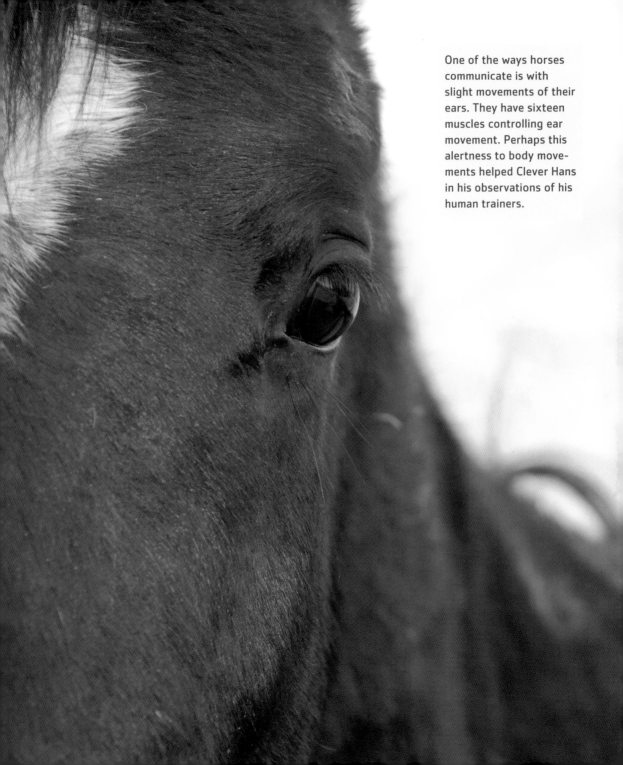

One of the ways horses communicate is with slight movements of their ears. They have sixteen muscles controlling ear movement. Perhaps this alertness to body movements helped Clever Hans in his observations of his human trainers.

to answer questions based on the tiny movements of the trainer or examiner. This ability to read the body language of the examiner became known as the Clever Hans Phenomenon.

Researchers now know that when working with a nonhuman animal, they must take measures to ensure that the Clever Hans Phenomenon doesn't happen during their study. The animal must not be able to pick up on any signals from the researchers that would alter their results. That's why owners are often blindfolded or asked to step out of the room when their dogs are being studied.

The Clever Hans Phenomenon is just one challenge facing animal cognition researchers during their experiments. There are many more. But let's begin the same way they do—with the scientific method and asking the right questions.

THE SCIENTIFIC METHOD

"For a scientist, knowing the questions to ask is as important as finding the answers," says Dr. Diana Reiss, a dolphin researcher.

Most questions begin with observations. Let's take a look at an early study that Dr. Reiss conducted as an example. She began by watching the dolphins swim and play together. She wanted to know more about how they communicated with each other and if humans might be able to communicate with a different species.

When Dr. Reiss began her studies it was common for researchers to use two methods. Some observed their subjects at set times, such as every hour or half-hour, and then selected behaviors from a list to describe their observations. That catalog of behaviors is called an *ethogram*.

Other researchers videotape their subjects and then analyze the recording back in their laboratory. Dr. Reiss didn't use either of these methods. She observed the dolphins in their natural setting and recorded their overall patterns of behavior. She was actually learning about them by being with them.

In most cases, before starting an experiment, scientists must come up with a hypothesis, or potential answer to their question. It's somewhere between a guess and a statement and similar to a prediction. In Dr. Reiss's case, she set out with the long-term goal of discovering what it is like for a dolphin to be a dolphin. Her short-term goal was to explore the cognitive abilities of dolphins through their communication.

A dolphin at the National Aquarium is studied by cognitive researchers.

Next, scientists design an experiment to validate that prediction. An experiment will have a series of steps that supply the data needed to make a conclusion. After spending time with the dolphins, Dr. Reiss set out to learn everything she could about dolphin communication. She located recording equipment, learned how to record sounds underwater, and spent time observing the dolphins. Then she began to record the dolphin sounds under the water.

The data that researchers collect may or may not support the initial hypothesis. At the end of Dr. Reiss's research she had a number of recordings of dolphin sounds to take back to her university for analysis. But she hadn't collected enough observations to support her hypothesis. There was not enough definitive data with which to make a conclusion.

Even if the data collected does support a hypothesis, researchers often aren't finished. Dr. Reiss's experiment, for example, left her with more questions. "A question answered usually raises new problems, and it would be presumptuous to assume that an end is ever achieved," said Dr. Karl von Frisch in his Nobel Prize Lecture.

Whatever the result of the experiment, the scientific method has helped grow the body of knowledge on that subject and created a new jumping-off point for other researchers. Dr. Reiss's study on dolphin communication was the first of many under her guidance and it led to important findings about how dolphins see themselves and the world around them.

WHO INVENTED THE SCIENTIFIC METHOD?

It's hard to tell who really invented the scientific method; it is very old. Before the nineteenth century, the method was referred to as the experimental method or the method of science. Regardless of the name, many have contributed to it. Aristotle (who was a scientist as well as a philosopher) and Roger Bacon (who used empirical methods in the thirteenth century) both had a hand in it. But it is Galileo, Francis Bacon, and René Descartes who began explaining a method of study for their scientific exploration and received the most ownership over its invention. Many others in the field of science and philosophy, including Charles Darwin, Gregor Mendel, Albert Einstein, and Marie Curie, later added to its development.

Galileo Galilei.

LITTLE FURRY PEOPLE

As researchers explore the minds of nonhuman animals they are warned not to insert human perceptions into their studies—traditionally a major taboo for those who study animal cognition and behavior.

For example, if we see a monkey holding a baby, we might assume that mom feels love toward her young. That would be projecting a human trait onto the behavior we are seeing. Or we might describe a vocalizing monkey as squealing with excitement. Picture animal characters like Stuart Little or Winnie-the-Pooh. Did you ever see a real mouse driving a car? Do bears live inside trees and eat honey from jars? Or talk to kangaroos and tigers? Nope. You can probably name a lot of other animals in books, movies, and cartoons that act like humans.

"Say a lion was stalking a zebra; if you said the lion wanted to catch it, you'd be accused of projecting your human emotions," said Dr. Carl Safina, writing of how inferring an animal's emotions, motivation, and awareness could stop a scientist's career. The term used for this human behavior is *anthropocentrism,* which means "putting humans at the center" of our thinking. This type of thinking can also border on *anthropomorphism,* as in the case of Winnie-the-Pooh, which means we think of our nonhuman neighbors as furry or scaly little people that act just like we do.

However, some valued researchers who have shaped our way of thinking about animals have been accused of committing the crime of anthropomorphism. Jane Goodall, for example, named her primate subjects during her studies in Gombe and was criticized for using the words *childhood* and *excitement* when making observations. Yet without Goodall's research, the science of animal behavior and cognition would not have moved forward in such a crucial way.

Researchers walk a fine line. It is important to recognize animals for what they are, even when we find them exhibiting behaviors similar to our own. We might find we have traits in common or that they have another meaning in that creature's world.

Safina strikes out at those who believe animals don't have emotions: "When someone says you can't attribute human emotions to animals, they forget the key leveling detail: humans *are* animals."

THE NOBLE BEAST

As difficult as it is to avoid thinking of animals as simply furry (or scaly, or feathered) people, we must not turn them into perfect, ideal creatures either. Observations show us that ants take slaves, monkeys steal, male lions have killed young cubs fathered by another lion, and elephants can be deceptive. Just like humans, these creatures are not perfect.

"At Gombe I thought the chimps were nicer than we are. But time has revealed that they can be just as awful," says Goodall.

THE INNER WORLD AND THE OUTER WORLD

Researchers face another challenge. Each animal has a world only it knows. When studying a species, researchers need to acknowledge and consider an animal's *umwelt* and *innenwelt,* two terms coined by German behaviorist Jakob von Uexküll in 1934. *Umwelt* describes the world surrounding an animal. *Innenwelt* refers to its world as it is perceived and internalized.

An animal's umwelt and innenwelt are unique to them. We perceive the world around us quite differently than an animal does. For example, dogs' naturally strong sense of smell powerfully affects how they comprehend the world. It provides them with a special awareness of the environment that we don't share. Dogs smell things we don't. Humans smell the strongest odor in the room, but a dog can smell even the faintest scents remaining from the previous day.

The same is true of other animals. Think about how an owl is able to stalk its prey on a dark night. Not only are its eyes large, but they have more rods and fewer cones than human eyes. This makes them lose color vision, but enables them to see a lot better in the dark.

"There are birds that see ultraviolet, insects that see infrared, many animals that see the polarization of sunlight, bats that hear sounds three octaves higher in pitch than the highest we hear and use sonar to 'see' the flapping of an insect's wings," writes Professor Clive D. L. Wynne in his book *Animal Cognition.*

All creatures perceive the world a bit differently than humans do because their senses work differently than ours. They might see different colors, have stronger hearing, or be able to see in the dark.

"We must first blow . . . a soap bubble around each creature to represent its own world, filled with the perceptions which it alone knows," wrote von Uexküll.

IN THE WILD

Studying animals in the wild raises other issues. Weather, politics, geography, and simply locating subjects play into a successful study in the wild. Think about how difficult it is for researchers to study large blue whales in the vast ocean or elusive tigers in dense Asian mangrove forests. Animals also cross borders. Scientists often need permission from multiple countries to research their subjects. They might also have to deal with poachers who are illegally killing or harming their subjects. Veterinary help might not be available in the wild as it is in a laboratory. Study activities might even cause a disturbance to the habitat or to other species.

It isn't easier when subjects are bred in captivity. Scientists have challenges there, too. Aside from basic care and feeding, they must make sure that the animals are safe during and after their study. They are always focused on their subjects' welfare.

THE THREE Rs

To deal with animal welfare challenges, experts have developed a strategy using the three Rs—replacement, reduction, and refinement. These address the ethical use of animals in science. Not all of these issues come up in cognition science, but they might in a laboratory setting. Scientists first examine the method of the study to see if it can be accomplished without the use of live animals (instead replacing them with something else, such as human volunteers or computer models). Reduction refers to using as few animals as necessary in the study. Refinement refers to modifying the study to minimize the stress on the animals.

Sometimes the challenges a researcher faces are more simple and obvious. Just ask Dr. Laurie Santos, who studies rhesus macaque monkeys in the wild. "Sometimes the monkeys just walk away and don't complete the study," she says as she squats down in front of a monkey on Cayo Santiago, an island off the coast of Puerto Rico.

Despite all of these challenges, researchers are making incredible discoveries in the field of animal cognition, as you'll see from Dr. Santos's work.

One of the free-ranging rhesus macaques that are descendants of the 409 that were brought to the island in 1938.

MAKING DECISIONS
MONKEY ISLAND

Dr. Laurie Santos waits with her fellow researchers on a pier that stretches out into the turquoise waters of the Caribbean Sea. It's seven a.m. when they board a small motorboat and set off for a private island just off the coast of Puerto Rico that's open only to researchers.

Despite the sunny morning, they are all wearing long pants, long-sleeved shirts, hiking boots, and brimmed hats. It's protocol. They are about to land on Monkey Island, also known as the Cayo Santiago Field Station, where rhesus macaques will outnumber them 1,000 to 20.

To protect the monkeys and the researchers from germs and disease, two buckets and a scrubber are on the pier. Everyone on the boat is to dip a boot

Protective clothing is essential in this field setting. Brimmed hats guard the researchers from more than the sun. These monkeys naturally carry the herpes B virus, which can be deadly to people. It's important not to be urinated on by an infected monkey in a tree above you!

The researchers and I sail off on the 7 a.m. boat to Monkey Island.

in bucket one, then scrub the boot bottom. Repeat with boot number two, then dip both in the second solution. When the researchers leave the island for the day they will repeat the process of cleaning their boots before they enter the boat for the return trip.

The boat arrives and after a quick ride they are on the island. It doesn't take long to spot a small young monkey peering from a tree branch. Soon there are hundreds clamoring for a meal of monkey chow. The sound of wind whipping through the island's palms is broken with monkey whistles and screeches as the top of the monkey hierarchy gets first dibs on the chow.

All of the researchers today have prepared their experiments in advance so that they can get the most out of their limited time on the island. Dr. Santos, of the Comparative Cognition Laboratory at Yale, studies the evolutionary origins of the human mind by comparing cognitive abilities of people and monkeys. The monkeys are not natural inhabitants of Cayo Santiago. They are the direct descendants of a group of 409 monkeys that were brought to the island in 1938 from India for research by Dr. Clarence Carpenter and the School of Tropical Medicine. The island and its monkeys are now maintained by two organizations: the Caribbean Primate Research Center and the University of Puerto Rico. Researchers vie for spots to study this special population.

A curious young macaque peeks at the researchers from up in a tree.

Rhesus macaques are classified as a species of Old World monkey. Although native to Asia, they can live in many places and many different habitats, including grasslands and forests. Many live close to humans, especially in India, where they are regarded as sacred. They live in noisy troops of up to two hundred individuals and are very social. The monkeys on the island are fed Purina monkey chow at three feeding stations to keep their diet steady. However, they also eat the island's leaves, fruits, flowers, and soil.

One of the large feeding areas for the monkeys on Cayo Santiago.

The first time Dr. Santos encountered the small, pink-faced monkeys, she was hooked. She tells the story of how one day she was sitting alone on the beach eating. A monkey came by and sat beside her with a piece of monkey chow. The two sat together eating. She began to wonder what he was thinking. "Did he think the spot was beautiful? And how would I know that he did? That got me thinking about how they're a lot like us, but on the other hand so different."

Santos makes no bones about it: human beings are smart. We think of ourselves as the top of the cerebral totem pole. But, she claims, "we can also be incredibly dumb on the aspects of our own decision making." For example, we tend to make very specific mistakes about such things as spending money, and we repeat them.

A baby monkey eating a piece of monkey chow.

"We pay too much attention to losses and this affects our ability to decide how much risk to take on in given situations. We also pay too much attention to price and confuse an item's price with its value," says Santos.

Think about the decisions you make when you receive money. Do you spend it? Do you save it? Do you gamble it away in the hopes that you may make more?

Enter the monkeys. Dr. Santos decided to explore the reasoning behind our own decisions through studying monkeys.

Monkeys are smart too. She's observed that they are capable of making decisions, such as which monkeys to hang out with, when to leave their group, and whom to mate with. Unlike us, though, Santos points out that they don't have the societal trappings of technologies and language that might mess them up like we do. She turned to a captive group of capuchin monkeys for this first laboratory experiment.

Santos wanted to see if the monkeys would make the same poor choices that humans commonly make. But monkeys don't use money! The first challenge she faced was creating a currency and teaching the monkeys how to use it.

MONKEYS AND MONEY

At first, the round piece of metal her team devised as "money" was useless to the monkeys. They had to learn that they could hand the token over to a researcher posing as a salesperson and they would get a treat. With very little training the monkeys became accomplished at using the token. Once they used it, Santos wanted to see if they would start to pay attention to their treat purchases and keep track of their tokens.

The monkeys discovered that they could purchase food treats for one token from a salesperson. Sometimes the salesperson sold more than one item per token. Other times the monkeys could buy better, tastier food with their token.

The results were surprising. The researchers discovered that the monkeys' behavior mimicked how people behave in dealing with currency. They took advantage of sales, when they could obtain more treats for the price of a token. They didn't save their tokens. And they stole tokens from each other. The next question was whether the monkeys would also make the same bad decisions. Would they risk their tokens? Would they act like humans do and try to avoid a loss?

Santos set up another experiment, this time with two salespeople. One offered the monkey a piece of apple for the price of one token, but surprise! When the monkey traded the token for the apple piece, it received a bonus piece of apple. So, the monkey got two pieces of apple for the price of one token. Happy monkey!

The second salesperson displayed three pieces of apple, but when the monkey gave him a token, the salesman took one piece away and gave only two pieces to the monkey.

In each transaction the monkey received two pieces of apple. Which salesperson do you think the monkeys returned to?

If you guessed that the monkeys returned to the salesman who gave them the bonus apple, you were right. It seems the monkeys would rather experience the bonus than experience a loss, even though they ended up with the same amount.

Each discovery Santos made led to more questions and more opportunities for further study. She continued with another experiment.

She introduced the monkeys to two salespeople who each offered the monkeys something different. The first displayed one grape, but gave a bonus with every token purchase, which meant the monkey always got two grapes. The other displayed one grape, but sometimes he gave three and sometimes just the one. Which will the monkeys choose? It turns out that monkeys, like humans, will play it safe and go with the salesperson who always does the same thing.

But Santos decided to go further in this experiment. She used the same two salespeople, but this time each one started out displaying three grapes. One of the salespeople always took one grape away, leaving two for the monkey. The other one sometimes took two away and sometimes only one.

Which did the monkeys choose? The monkeys always preferred to deal with the salesperson who gave them a bonus and avoided the one who gave them what looked like a loss. In this last experiment they were dealing with two types of loss—one was constant (one grape was always taken away) and the other involved risk (they didn't know whether one or two grapes would be removed). The monkeys chose the salesperson who offered more risk. They were willing to risk losing more because sometimes they wouldn't lose anything. That is exactly how humans behave.

Dr. Santos's experiments showed that if we give monkeys a currency, they act as we do, treating losses more importantly than gains. We've answered our first question—where do these judgment fluctuations come from? They may be due to our evolutionary history. They might be 35 million years old and have existed in our prehuman ancestors. That makes them hard to overcome.

GAMBLING APES

Alexandra Rosati, a researcher at Yale University, has been studying the role of emotion in decision making by introducing chimpanzees and bonobos to "gambling." "But it was not known if these processes are shared with other animals when they make decisions about their important resources—such as food," she told the *Daily Mail.*

Both the chimps and the bonobos were very upset when they lost after they "gambled" their treats for a better treat. Two of the chimps threw tantrums when they lost. They even tried to give back their treat selection in an effort to have a "do-over." Rosati believes that this behavior sheds some light on "why we humans make the decisions we do."

Psychologists and economists have found that emotions play a critical role in shaping how humans make complex decisions, such as those that involve saving, gambling, or investing money.

Dr. Rosati believes that apes make decisions based on moods and motivations, just like us.

"If you see something in a primate," says Santos, "you can use it as a window into the evolutionary past of human beings."

This is not meant to be discouraging. Dr. Santos likes to remind us that not only are humans smart, we are also very good at overcoming our biological limitations. Thus it is important for us to recognize them, so that we can overcome them.

Our primate brains are indeed complex, but how they work in making decisions and solving problems can be seen in a creature we usually consider so low on the cerebral totem pole, it might just surprise you.

Let's take a look at the tiny honeybee.

THE DANCE OF THE HONEYBEE

Thinking of a swarm of honeybees as a collective brain that can make good decisions might seem like something out of a sci-fi movie, but this way of thinking is actually a major scientific breakthrough.

In 1944 Dr. Karl von Frisch, professor of zoology at the University of Munich in Germany, made a discovery that later earned him a Nobel Prize. He found that a worker honeybee was capable of informing her hive where to find a valued source of food by dancing. He already knew about the "waggle" dance she performed when she returned to the hive. But up until 1944, he believed she was only sharing the fragrance of the flowers she had visited.

His discovery was that the activity was not a scent dance. The bee was actually sharing location information, like a dancing GPS service. The bee's

Dr. Seeley learned that honeybees not only communicate about food sources, but also democratically make decisions.

dance was a reenactment of her recent flight. Although this was a ground-breaking discovery, an even greater one was on the horizon.

The young graduate student he was supervising, Martin Lindauer, continued von Frisch's studies with the honeybees into the 1950s. Since then, the Cornell University biologist Dr. Thomas Seeley and others have taken the studies further, learning that these honeybee swarms not only communicate about food sources, but also democratically decide where to build a new hive. Now we're talking about a collective brain! There's our breakthrough discovery!

Can this decision-making process be compared to how primates make

Sometimes returning to an experiment yields very different results, as in this example from Frisch's 1973 Nobel Lecture. As he redid the experiment he found that it was not fragrance, but location that the bees were communicating. Like any good scientist, he continued asking questions and testing theories. "This was how things stood in 1923, and I believed I knew the language of the bees," he said. "On resuming the experiments twenty years later, I noticed that the most beautiful aspect had escaped me. Then, for the first time, I installed the feeding place several hundred meters away instead of next to the hive, and saw to my astonishment that the recruits immediately started foraging at that great distance while paying hardly any attention to the bowls near the hive."

decisions? Is there a similarity between swarms and human brains? Let's step back for a moment and look at how a primate brain makes a decision.

THE HIVE BRAIN

Our brains are filled with neurons that are constantly transferring information. Primate brains, including those of Dr. Santos's rhesus macaques as well as humans, make decisions by committee. This means that options are weighed and members pipe up about the choices. Eventually, everyone agrees on an action. Of course, this committee is not made up of little people; it's composed of neurons in your brain. So in many ways our brain acts like a hive. Maybe you've heard the term *hive mind* or *swarm intelligence* when referring to getting consensus among a group of people. It's also the reason a school of fish can outsmart a predator.

Dr. Seeley explored this idea with a honeybee experiment. His team set up honeybee swarms on an island that didn't have any natural nests. Two nesting boxes were set up: one was an ideal box and the other needed a little work.

Scout bees took off for both sites. The researchers collected the scout bees that visited the two hive sites. All the bees that visited one were marked with yellow paint and the bees that visited the other were marked with pink paint.

Each color represented a different hive site and a different option or possibility. Each site had its different characteristics. Which hive site would the bees decide on? Both yellow- and pink-marked bees performed waggle dances to spread the word about what they found.

Seeley and his team found that in addition to the dance, the bees in the swarm head-butted the dancing bees as a signal to stop dancing. "The head butting serves in discouraging support of the other site. It's all about which site will get the critical level of popularity first," says Seeley.

They discovered that each bee marked with one color would head butt a bee marked with the other color when it danced. So pink would head butt yellow and vice versa. As more scouts went out to see the sites, one color became more dominant.

"Honeybee swarms and complex brains show many parallels in how they make decisions," wrote Seeley and his research team in their 2012 paper for *Science*.

Imagine yourself making the decision between eating ice cream or a salad. Some of your brain neurons will fire for each, while others will try to stop neurons from firing. There is both positive and negative signaling until

Douglas Hofstadter wrote in his book *Gödel, Escher, Bach: An Eternal Golden Braid*, "Ant colonies are no different from brains in many respects." He compared individual ants acting within the community to neurons in the brain of a higher organism performing in a perfect democratic process.

a consensus is reached and the brain—you—makes the decision on which to eat.

Now picture each neuron as a little bee and you have a hive. A brain built of neurons. A swarm built of bees. Both are thinking machines.

We make decisions every day. Some have a lot of thought behind them and others, not so much, but they make us into the people we are. How we treat people, for instance, may be almost automatic or may involve long deliberations about the right way to act. Those are known as moral decisions. They often indicate our humanness. Researchers are finding that animals also make moral decisions. Let's take a look.

Honey bees on a honeycomb with the queen bee in the middle.

EMOTIONS AND EMPATHY
WALKING IN SOMEONE ELSE'S SHOES

Imagine that you are reading a terrific book and you know your friend would love it too. Would you share it with your friend when you are done? You might, because you believe your friend would also enjoy it.

But would you share something like it, perhaps a favorite toy, if you were two years old? In the early years of our life we are focused primarily on ourselves and our own needs. As we grow and develop, we recognize the needs of others. Sharing is a common human trait.

Recognizing what someone else might desire or perceiving their emotions is what psychologists call *theory of mind*, similar to the ability to "put yourself in someone else's shoes."

THEORY OF MIND

Although some of her work takes place in a laboratory, Dr. Santos has been visiting Cayo Santiago and learning from its wild monkey population every year since 1993. She is interested in finding out more about how these monkeys think and if they are able to display theory of mind.

Even as recently as a couple of decades ago, scientists doubted that chimpanzees, who are more closely related to humans than monkeys are, had

"I think that the rat's mind and the man's mind are the same machine, but of unequal capacities—like yours and Edison's." —Mark Twain

Dr. Santos has been conducting experiments on Cayo Santiago since 1993.

this skill. So how could monkeys have it? But Santos's work on the island has been changing this view.

Santos set up a theory of mind experiment to test whether monkeys assume that people will guard their food just like monkeys do. Santos's theory was that the monkeys would prefer to steal from people who are looking away—that is, when the food is not well guarded.

She began her experiment by searching for a test subject—a monkey who wasn't busy and who wasn't being distracted by other monkeys. It took some time because the island is crowded with busy monkeys!

Once she had the attention of a monkey, she held up two grapes for it to see. She poked each grape onto a stick and had one of her graduate students stand behind each stick. One student stared straight ahead and the other

Monkeys will steal from researchers if they know the researcher isn't watching.

looked away. In six experiments, the monkeys stole the grape from the student who wasn't looking at the grape rather than the one who was facing the monkey (and the grape). This indicates that the monkeys were taking into account where the student was looking, and then guessing whether the student knew he was about to steal the grape.

According to Santos, these results suggest that rhesus macaques possess an essential component of theory of mind, which is the ability to figure out what others perceive on the basis of where they are looking. The monkeys not only follow the gaze of the researchers, they also understand what others know.

That capacity of getting into someone else's mind also gives us the ability to perceive what it means to be someone else.

BONOBOS SHARE WITH STRANGERS

Dr. Brian Hare, a professor at Duke University, conducted an experiment with bonobos, who are genetically closer to humans than monkeys are. Hare and his research team conducted experiments with bonobos living at the Lola ya Bonobo Sanctuary in the Democratic Republic of Congo. They started with the knowledge that humans share with others, even with strangers. It was thought that this feature was unique to humans because of our use of language and social behavior. Hare and his team wanted to see if bonobos possess this trait as well.

They placed three bonobos in three separate enclosures near each other. The bonobo in the center enclosure knew one of the other bonobos, but the other was a stranger. The center bonobo knew how to open the door of the other two enclosures.

A pile of food was provided in a test room. The center bonobo could enter the room and eat all the food or invite the other bonobos to share.

Researchers reported that in more than 70 percent of the trials of this experiment, the center bonobo shared the food at least once. Additional experiments showed that bonobos would share food with a strange bonobo if they were able to engage in some social interaction before the sharing opportunity, but not if no social interaction was possible with the new bonobo. Their results demonstrate that the bonobos do care about others, but unlike humans, they won't give without some interaction. Humans will give anonymously without any personal interaction. That might mean sending funds

to people in crisis or making a donation of clothing in one of those metal bins outside a store. Humans don't need to know who will actually receive their donation, but that is not the case with the bonobos. They require interaction for their act of generosity.

However, despite their need for association, the bonobos do share. But monkeys and bonobos are primates, close relatives to humans. Can other animals that are far more distantly related feel empathy, share, and exhibit the traits of theory of mind?

Dr. Hare also studies dog cognition. Through his research he has shown that dogs could look at him, understand that he had information about hidden food, and find the food when he pointed to it. This wouldn't surprise most dog owners. Is that theory of mind, or conditioning? Hare believes it is theory of mind.

Sometimes surprising animal stories pop up in the news. These stories can give us another glimpse into the minds of animals, even though they exist outside of a controlled study.

SHARING AND CARING

Lilica is a Brazilian stray dog whose behavior has made the news. She walks miles through the streets of São Carlos, São Paulo, to visit dog lover Lucia Helena de Souza each night. The woman leaves out a bag of food and Lilica takes it and travels back to her home in a junkyard. She doesn't touch a bite of the food until she arrives at her home, where she shares it with the other animals—a dog, a cat, a mule, and a few chickens—that also live in the junkyard.

De Souza had no idea what was going on with this hungry dog until she followed her one night. She found that the stray dog had puppies to feed, but soon she was feeding the other animals there too. Even when de Souza arranged to have her puppies adopted into homes, Lilica still visited her house each night and brought a food bag home for her animal neighbors to share.

Elephants, too, don't need to be related to help each other. The zoologist Ian Douglas-Hamilton and his team of researchers recorded an incident they witnessed in 2003 in Kenya's Samburu National Reserve.

Eleanor, a dying elephant matriarch on a Kenyan game reserve, had a swollen trunk. She dragged it along the ground, and then fell to the ground. Minutes later Grace, another matriarch from a different group, approached Eleanor and lifted her back on her feet. Grace tried to help her walk, but Eleanor fell again. Grace didn't give up. She continued to push and nudge Eleanor with her tusks.

These examples happened naturally, without the intervention of scientists. We can learn from observing them. They speak to the fact that humans may not be the only creatures that can be kind to others.

"I am not even particularly interested in demonstrating animal empathy, because for me the critical issue is no longer whether they have it, but how it works," says Dr. Frans de Waal, a well-known primatologist at Emory University.

EMO RATS

Picture this: Two rats, one trapped in a plastic tube, the other free to wander around. Next to the trapped rat is another tube, but instead of holding a rat, it's filled with five chocolate chips, something rats *love* to eat. What do you think will happen next? Can you develop your own hypothesis?

"I think that the rat's mind and the man's mind are the same machine, but of unequal capacities—like yours and Edison's," speculated Mark Twain about the minds of animals in his book *What Is Man*.

Dr. Peggy Mason, an animal cognitive researcher from the University of Chicago, had her own theory about rat brains. Could she prove that rats, although despised by many people, have the cognitive ability to show empathy? She, along with researchers Dr. Jean Decety and Dr. Inbal Ben-Ami Bartal, conducted the experiment with the two rats, one trapped and one free.

The free rat saw the trapped rat and moved over to the plastic tube. It

Dr. Bartal and Dr. Mason observing two rats during their study.

sniffed around the plastic. It explored the openings. The trapped rat scratched furiously at the plastic, trying to get out. The free rat continued to study the tube. Rather than enter the other tube with the chocolate chips and have a feast, it spent its time working to free the trapped rat. Once it was able to free the trapped rat, it moved on to the chocolate chips.

Do you think it ate them all? It didn't. It ate three and a half and left the rest for the other rat. Pretty amazing, right?

Do you think that the free rat felt empathy for the trapped rat? Peggy Mason and her team believe it did. This is very different from the primitive form of empathy called *emotional contagion* that scientists previously believed rats experienced. Scientists had proven that if a rat saw another rat in distress, it too would feel distress. The team wanted to see if a rat would actually work to help a comrade. The rat that helped the trapped rat didn't experience visible stress behavior such as grinding its teeth or chattering.

So what does this mean? One important finding is that empathy-driven behavior isn't unique to us. It might also prove that we humans are "biologically mandated to be empathetically concerned and helping," according to Mason. This trait may have evolved as part of human nature, starting with our early beginnings as mammals. We are hard-wired, just like a computer, to behave in this way. Mason also suggests that humans should act on this "biological inheritance" more often.

TIME TO FORGIVE

Let's head to the lunchroom. You're sitting with your friends and before you know it, you are having an argument. It stretches into the rest of the day and you leave school feeling bad. What do you do? You probably would want to make things right again. Wouldn't you?

Dr. Frans de Waal conducted a study on aggression and competition among chimpanzees. He made conclusions during this investigation that deep down, animals, including humans, are competitors and act with aggression. In fact, he wrote an entire book focused on this research called *Our Inner Ape*. But he made another observation that led him to other paths of research. He observed that the chimpanzees reconciled after they had fights.

He watched two males in a tree after a fight. One of them held out his hand to the other. Seconds later they came together, kissed, and embraced each other.

"The principle is that you have a valuable relationship that is damaged by conflict, so you need to do something about it," said de Waal.

Further studies led to more observations. De Waal watched as a male chimp screamed after losing a fight with another chimp. A younger one came over to the chimp in distress and put an arm around him to calm him down. The younger chimp was consoling the other chimp. This behavior is driven by empathy. It's very similar to behavior observed with human children within their family.

Vicky Horner, a researcher at Emory University in Georgia, conducted an experiment to examine whether chimpanzees are indifferent to the welfare of others, as was believed. She displayed two color tokens to two chimpanzees and gave one the ability to choose from the two. If the chimp chose the red token, the chimp would get a food reward. If the chimp chose the green token, both chimps would get food rewards. Which do you think the chimp chose? The researchers found that the chimps actually preferred the prosocial green token that fed them both.

They also observed that if the partner put a little pressure on the chimp that was choosing, like spitting water on it or intimidating it, then the choosing chimp would not pick the token that would give them both a reward.

Chimpanzees, our closest relative, share 98 percent of our genetic makeup. Like monkeys and other primates, they live in social groups. They stand 4 to 5 1/2 feet tall (1.2–1.7 meters) and are part of the great ape family of primates. Unfortunately, these intelligent creatures are endangered due to habitat loss, disease, and hunting. They have already disappeared from four African countries. One recent Ivory Coast census found that the chimp population had decreased by 90 percent over the last twenty years.

Does this remind you of any experiences you have in the human world? It probably does!

Following studies found that these altruistic actions vary between wild and laboratory settings, and between genders. As in most research, each discovery leads to more questions and more avenues of study.

"For me, the most important find is that like us, chimpanzees take into account the needs and wishes of others," says Horner.

De Waal speaks of the pillars of morality as being compassion and fairness: "One is reciprocity, and associated with it is a sense of justice and a sense of fairness. And the other one is empathy and compassion."

We've explored empathy and compassion; now let's see how justice and fairness are established in the animal kingdom.

EXPLORE THE YAWN CONTAGION

Have you noticed that when someone yawns, you feel like yawning too? That's known as the yawn contagion, meaning the yawn is contagious, like a cold. It's catching. Dr. Frans de Waal has done experiments with monkeys and found that they will also yawn if they see another monkey yawning. The yawn contagion is tied to empathy. It's been observed that people with a high yawn contagion are the most empathetic. Experiment with this yourself.

Just like humans, dogs do not like to be treated unfairly.

FAIRNESS
EVERYONE LIKES FAIR TREATMENT

Nobody likes to feel slighted. You know how you'd feel if everyone in your class was invited to a party except for you. Feeling slighted is universal to humans. We've all been there and we all know it doesn't feel good.

Scientists refer to our dislike of not being treated fairly as *inequity aversion*. There are two types. The first is when we see others receive more than we do, like being the only one not invited to a party. The second is when we notice we are receiving more than the people around us. Now imagine you did get invited to that party, but you feel bad because your best friend didn't.

Researchers are exploring whether animals can recognize when they are not treated fairly and experience inequity. Since we are not the only social animals, it is likely that we are not the only animals who shy away from inequity.

DOGS FEEL JEALOUSY

Anyone who owns a dog and has welcomed another dog into the family has probably observed a moment when one dog is treated differently than the other. Does the dog notice? How does it react?

Dr. Friederike Range, senior scientist and head of the Clever Dog Lab and co-director of Wolf Science Center in Austria, conducted an experiment.

She asked Guinness, a fluffy black and white dog, to give her paw, which the dog did. She didn't reward Guinness with anything, but the dog was quick to continue the response pattern. Over and over again Range asked for her paw and Guinness offered it without a problem.

Range then brought in another dog, Guinness's pal Toddy. Toddy was also asked for his paw. When he gave it, Range rewarded him with a treat in front of Guinness.

Subject refusing to look at the experimenter while declining to give paw.

"Of jealousy in dogs innumerable instances might be given, but I shall merely quote one," wrote Charles Darwin. He told the story of an old Scottish terrier that spent a lot of time "following, watching, and imitating" a younger rival dog who was brought into the house. He ate when the younger dog ate, wanted to go out when the younger dog went out, and "[burst] out whining and barking" when the other dog was petted and he wasn't.

Guinness was asked for her paw again, and when she offered it, she didn't receive a reward. After this pattern was repeated a few more times, Guinness began to whimper. Then she went on strike. No more paw giving.

Range believed that Guinness understood that she was being wronged and predicted what she was thinking: *Why should I work for free when he's getting rewarded?*

Range repeated this experiment with dozens of other dogs and observed the same results.

Dogs have been living with humans for so long that they have been shaped by how we have bred them. This has given them a unique intelligence and an overwhelming desire to be close to humans.

"Such jealousy seems to me a very advanced emotion, as it has passed beyond the stage when it may be supposed to be caused by a fear of other animals monopolizing material benefits which they desire for themselves; it is excited solely by seeing affection or attention bestowed by those they love upon other animals," wrote Darwin.

Jealousy and justice are very close. "If a master is not equal in his ways towards his dogs, the dogs are very apt to discover the injustice and to resent it accordingly."

Capuchin monkeys are tiny, weighing only three to nine pounds (1.4–4 kilograms). They can be found in parts of South America and Latin America, where they live in trees in large groups. Capuchins are often used in primate studies because they are clever and easy to train.

MONKEYS GET JEALOUS TOO!

Dr. Sarah Brosnan, a psychologist, and Dr. Frans de Waal explored moral fairness with a group of brown capuchin monkeys. They put two of the monkeys together. The monkeys are part of the same group, so they know each other. The researchers then give them a task. Each monkey has to hand over a stone to get a food reward. The reward is a piece of cucumber. Both do this over and over without a problem.

Then the researchers change it up. They give one monkey a piece of cucumber and the other a more desirable treat—a grape. The first monkey notices this but still returns the stone—and again receives cucumber. Clearly there is inequity here. What does the monkey do?

The monkeys "don't necessarily have to have an idea of fairness or an idea of the way the world should work. All they have to care about is they got less than someone else," says Dr. Brosnan.

The monkey throws the cucumber back at the researcher and pulls on the cage bars. Not pleased! She is handed another stone and taps it against the wall to test it out. She then hands it to the researcher, who rewards her with another piece of cucumber. Meanwhile, the other monkey has been receiving grapes for every transaction. Monkey number one is not pleased and again throws the cucumber at the researcher. Clearly she is not being treated fairly.

These findings point to an early evolutionary origin of recognizing inequity. Our need for equal pay for equal work may go back to our early beginnings. Brosnan concludes that animals have complex social rules similar to those of humans.

In further experiments Brosnan worked with other monkey pairings and found that some monkeys receiving the grapes would stop giving the stones in protest of the monkey who wasn't being treated fairly. This points even more closely to our human behavior.

Dr. Clive Wynne, professor of psychology at the University of Florida, has another thought. He points to the frustration we feel when we don't get what we want. It's the same reason a child might throw a tantrum. Other animal species share this frustration with us. Maybe it isn't justice, but a feeling of frustration or greed that is motivating this behavior. Regardless of how you look at it, Brosnan insists that both echo human behavior.

Monkeys and dogs are social animals. Researchers believe other social animals, like lions and wolves, might also experience inequity aversion. We'll just have to wait for the results of those experiments.

Dr. Sarah Brosnan doing an exchange with a male brown capuchin monkey (*Cebus [Sapajus] apella*) named Liam. He's in the test box and has just returned the orange cube token in her left hand and is taking the grape from her right hand.

COMMUNICATION
NEIGHBORHOOD TALK

While walking the path onto Monkey Island, you will hear rustling wind, squawking birds overhead, and the babble and squeaks of the island's monkeys. These sounds are unique to this place. Every place has its own sounds. This island in the Caribbean does not sound the same as the old-growth forests of the Pacific Northwest. And your backyard does not sound the same as someone else's. Each place has its own neighborhoods and its own chatty inhabitants.

The sounds we hear are animals and insects communicating in subtle and complex ways. Crickets rub their wings together to create a song. Black bears use body and facial expressions along with whines, snorts, and roars. Birds use a variety of sounds, calls, and positions to communicate.

The rhesus macaques on the island use coos, grunts, screeches, squeaks, growls, barks, and warbles to communicate, but they can also be seen making facial gestures, such as baring their teeth, and body postures.

Just like us, animals utilize vocabulary, grammar, accents, and gestures. They also communicate with vision, smell, touch, or taste as well as sounds. We humans must look past our own facial and bodily expressions to signals involving any or all of the senses when we are trying to understand how animals communicate. Whether they are "speaking" in squawks, barks, hoots,

Up until recently scientists believed that humans were the only animals that had specific labels or names for each other. Now we know that dolphins do also.

or whistles, or touching an iPad screen, information is passing from one animal to another.

IS THAT YOU?

If your mom entered your classroom and began speaking with your teacher, you would recognize her voice without even looking up from your work. Recognizing the sounds of our own species is important not only for social interactions; it is also a matter of survival. All animals need to know if another animal is angry or friendly. But what happens in our primate brain when we hear different sounds? Researchers wanted to know.

They conducted a study in 2008 using macaques. They sedated the monkeys and put them in a magnetic resonance imaging (MRI) scanner. The MRI is a diagnostic machine that uses magnetic fields and radio waves to create an image of a body's organs and bones; in this case, it focused on the macaques' brains. The scan is painless, but you have to lie very still while a

Rhesus macaques communicate with coos, growls, barks, and other vocalizations. Like humans they respond more readily to the sounds of each other than other creatures.

large tube-shaped magnet temporarily aligns the hydrogen atoms in your body to produce the image. The monkeys were strapped into special little chairs to hold them still.

It was found that the monkeys have a voice-sensitive area of their brain similar to that of humans. This area responded more to the voices of other macaques than to other species or environment sounds.

Monkeys are closely related to us; dogs are not. But if you own a dog, you know that its ears perk up when it hears your voice. This is easy for us to observe. Recently scientists wanted to find out what was going on inside those canine brains when they hear a human voice or a canine bark.

Hungarian scientists at the MR Research Center in Budapest trained a group of golden retrievers and border collies to lie absolutely still in an MRI scanner for a full six minutes while they played recordings of people shouting, crying, and laughing in 2014. The dogs were amazing test subjects. They seemed to enjoy the scan as they eagerly took their turn inside the MRI machine.

While the dogs were in the MRI they heard various human sounds, excluding speech. The researchers also played the sounds of dogs angrily barking and playfully yipping. They recorded the results of the dogs' brain activity.

The researchers compared the canine scans to human scans. The dogs did respond to the sounds in a similar area of the brain where humans show a response. Dogs and humans have regions of the brain dedicated to processing voices. Not surprisingly, both dogs and humans responded strongly to positive emotion sounds like laughter and a playful bark.

Like all research, the results led to more questions. Does this brain activity help dogs tune in to the feelings of their owners? Does it help humans tune in to the feelings of their dogs? Does this skill date back to a common ancestor of humans and dogs? Perhaps dogs react to our emotions because they were bred by humans, but it is believed that their capacity for understanding was already advanced before they became our pets.

DOLPHINESE

Animals squeak, squawk, and bark out their calls to one another, and recognize the calls of their own species. Dolphins go one step further with their

Dr. John Lilly supported the theory that human language developed in children through constant contact with their mothers. He decided to create an experiment to apply this same theory to dolphins. Lilly's research assistant, twenty-three-year-old Margaret Howe Lovatt, lived with a dolphin named Peter for ten weeks in 1965. The two shared a partially flooded house in the Virgin Islands that looked like any other villa on the island. Lovatt even slept on a bed that was soaked in salt water. This relationship became controversial because Peter did not accept Lovatt as a mother. Instead he wanted a mate. The relationship between Lovatt and Peter began to overshadow Lilly's communication research. The study did not end well and Lilly lost his funding.

communication skills. They not only whistle calls to each other, but also have been found to have their own signature whistles.

Neuroscientist Dr. John Lilly began his studies of dolphins back in the 1950s. His claims of dolphin intelligence excited the public, but his experiments grew controversial and he lost his credibility with his peers and the public. Unfortunately, dolphin language study was lost in the process. It became an off-limits subject among scientists until the Kewalo Basin Marine Mammal Laboratory was opened in Hawaii in 1970.

At John Lilly's urging, Dr. Diana Reiss visited Betty Brothers who fed dolphins from her dock. This led to her first study on dolphin communication. Here she is swimming with Delphi and Pan in her first lab in California soon after.

Someday scientists hope to have a box with all the building blocks of dolphin sound that can then be translated into symbols that will allow researchers to communicate with these intelligent mammals.

Studies now find that dolphins use signature whistles to identify and call one another. It has also been shown that they can identify each other's signature whistles years after they have been in contact with each other. Scientists believe that each dolphin calf invents its own whistle and keeps it for life—just like having your own individual name. Signature whistles are just some of the vocal sounds dolphins use in their communication.

Says the comparative psychologist Stan Kucaj, "The question is not how smart are dolphins, but how are dolphins so smart?"

"Scientists are now studying dolphins and let us hope that we someday will have a more intimate relationship with one of the most intelligent and friendly creatures, which may even help us to communicate with other forms of life. And who knows what frontier this might lead to." I wrote that in 1976 when I was in middle school in the conclusion of my report on dolphins. Little did I know then that I'd be writing this book as an adult or how far we would come in our research.

DOCTOR DOLITTLE

"Yes, there ARE plenty," said Polynesia. "But none of them are any good at all. Now listen, Doctor, and I'll tell you something. Did you know that animals can talk?"

Polynesia, Hugh Lofting's famous fictional talking parrot in his book *Doctor Dolittle*, spoke "over two thousand languages, including Dodo and Unicorn." Polynesia teaches the literary veterinarian how to communicate with every fish, fowl, and mammal, including Chee Chee, his monkey.

The world has been going on now for thousands of years, hasn't it? And the only thing in animal-language that PEOPLE have learned to understand is that when a dog wags his tail he means "I'm glad!"—It's funny, isn't it? You are the very first man to talk like us. (Polynesia to Doctor Dolittle in Doctor Dolittle by Hugh Lofting, 1920)

Hugh Lofting's multilingual veterinarian stepped off the page and onto the screen in 1967 and then again in 1998. It seems that every generation enjoys imagining a human who can "speak" to the animals.

DOCTOR DOLITTLE'S RETURN

BY HUGH LOFTING

Imagine speaking with animals and understanding everything they say, whether bark or squeal. Doctor Dolittle might be fictional, but communicating with other species is a very real possibility. In fact, there have already been animals that have been able to communicate with humans.

SIGNING PRIMATES

Koko, Washoe, and Nim are primates who have learned sign language to communicate their wants and needs. All have become very famous, but they've also been the subject of a lot of controversy.

Koko, a female lowland gorilla, was taught American Sign Language (ASL) over forty years ago by the psychologist Francine Patterson. Born on the Fourth of July in 1971, Koko is short for Hanabiko, Japanese for "fireworks child."

Koko's trainer claims that Koko now knows over a thousand signs that are a variation of ASL and can also understand roughly two thousand English verbal words. She's met many famous people over the years, including the actors Leonardo DiCaprio and Robin Williams. Perhaps one of her most interesting visits was from Jane Goodall in 1978. After Goodall returned to Africa, she wrote to Koko asking for advice for her studies with chimpanzees. Koko's advice was to approach the chimpanzees in a kneeling or crouching position, advice Goodall used in her research.

Washoe was born in West Africa in the 1960s. The chimpanzee was captured and brought to America, where University of Nevada psychologists Allen and

Beatrix Gardner adopted her. They raised her as a human child and gave her all the things a human child would need—books, clothing, even a toothbrush. They claimed she learned over 250 signs to communicate with them.

Another chimpanzee, Nim Chimpsky, was named after the famous linguist Noam Chomsky, who pioneered a theory that language was uniquely human. Evidence suggested that this chimpanzee's signing was just imitating his trainers. Was it an example of the Clever Hans Phenomenon?

Some wonder if the signing skills of these three great apes were an example of conditioning. Animal cognition experts recognize that these apes do communicate, but question their motivation. We humans chat together for fun; just picture your lunch table conversations or text messages. But apparently, apes don't. They sign only to communicate their needs. The human communication pattern is different.

In the 1930s, long before Koko, Nim, and Washoe were born, Winthrop Kellogg, an Indiana University psychologist, acquired a seven-and-a-half-month-old female chimpanzee named Gua and attempted to raise her alongside his human son, Donald. Gua learned to respond to Kellogg's verbal commands but never learned to speak. The experiment ended in just nine months. Others brought apes into their homes, including Dr. Maurice Temerlin, a psychotherapist and professor at the University of Oklahoma, and his wife, who raised a chimp named Lucy until she was about eleven years old. She learned about 250 signs in their care.

INTERSPECIES COMMUNICATION

A ladder leans up against the side of a cement building in Iowa. Waiting at the top is a view of something you won't see unless you travel to Africa—a bonobo habitat. A researcher stands on the roof holding a container full of grapes and bananas.

Stella, a research assistant at the Ape Cognition and Conservation Initiative, calls out, "Maisha, come on. I have a banana for you."

We wait. Maisha, whose name means "life" in Swahili, doesn't come out. Stella calls out again. Finally, after a little more coaxing, a young teenage bonobo, covered in thick black fur, enters our view. Stella tosses down a banana and a human-like hand snatches it up. Maisha moves quickly to a wooden structure and turns his back to eat his banana in private.

The view from the roof of the Ape Cognition and Conservation Initiative.

We leave him and walk across the roof. Three other male bonobos have access to this side. Thirty-six-year-old Kanzi, five-year-old Teco, and teenage Nyota. These three don't need much coaxing. Nyota, whose name means "star" in Swahili, comes running out at a fast clip, two legs and one arm

Maisha munches on her banana in a structure on the ACCI grounds.

moving quickly along the ground, and the other hand holding his laminated lexigram sheet, sliding it along as you would use a saucer sled to slide on the snow.

Nyota isn't the only bonobo using the lexigram sheet. After the bonobos receive their banana and grape treats outside, we climb back down the ladder and go inside to watch Kanzi and Nyota use this unique communication system.

Moments later we watch Kanzi, whose name means "treasure" in Swahili, jump up in front of his computer screen and turn it on by touching the large green dot in the center of the screen. Lexigrams appear on the screen. Similar to Egyptian hieroglyphs, lexigrams are symbols that represent words and things. Each lexigram is carefully designed and generally has nothing to do with the item it represents. They are created with specific colors and lines.

Nyota takes off with his lexigram chart.

Kanzi is able to use the lexigrams to communicate with humans. We watch as he points to the lexigram that symbolizes grapes. Kanzi wants grapes. Kanzi understands about three hundred lexigrams, and many more human spoken words. Communicating with Kanzi is unlike any other experience I've had with a nonhuman animal. It's not like we are having a conversation as we would with a friend, but it's clear that he understands what we are saying. Just like the other apes that are using sign language, Kanzi and the other bonobos don't chat about visitors or the weather; they respond to questions and communicate their needs.

Bonobo celebrity Kanzi at work at the lexigram screen.

But that doesn't mean that Kanzi only points to what he wants. Kanzi and Nyota have demonstrated higher-level thinking by being able to put lexigrams together. For example, Kanzi put the lexigrams for "slow" and "lettuce" together to describe kale (it took him a long time to chew kale!). He also put the lexigrams for "big" and "water" together during a time when the area was flooded. Nyota has put together the lexigrams "quiet" and "think" for communicating "Let's have some quiet time together."

What do you pack for a visit to a bonobo? It took me a while to figure out what I wanted to take to Kanzi and the other bonobos. I decided on a pinwheel, a magnet in the shape of New York State, a New York State blue bandanna, boxes of maple candies, organic grapes, bananas, an orange, and an apple. The bonobos would be able to see what I brought, but the fruit would have to be washed before they could receive it. We sat in front of the glass window and pulled out item after item. I found out that the bonobos' diet didn't allow for candy anymore, so those would be enjoyed by the human staffers. Kanzi gave a high-pitched whoop of excitement as each item came out of the bag. I knew he was happy, and I also knew that he understood that I had brought them. So why not lean into the glass to give sweet Kanzi a kiss? Because Kanzi likes to trick. Unlike Nyota, who puts his face close to the glass and keeps it there for the kiss, Kanzi acts like he will do the same, but as soon as you move your face close to the glass, a bonobo hand reaches out quickly to slap it. Kanzi, the trickster!

We watch as Teco, just like the youngster he is, competes with Kanzi for the space near the lexigram screen. Teco is already learning his lexigrams and is responding to spoken English.

The possibility of interspecies communication was scoffed at for many years. In 1980, just three years after Irene Pepperberg purchased Alex, the New York Academy of Sciences held a conference entitled "The Clever Hans Phenomenon: Communications with Horses, Whales, Apes, and People." Dr. Diana Reiss attended and was shocked at what she heard. A divide had formed between experts who trained performing animals for circuses and magic shows and researchers working in ape-language and interspecies communication. Many language researchers found themselves under fire. According to Susan Fowler, editor of the magazine *Lab Animal,* the conference was an "unprofessional, unpleasant attempt on the part of a semiotics professor to discredit the whole area of ape/human communication research."

Thomas A. Sebeok, director of the Research Center for Language and Semiotics Studies of Indiana University, who had planned the conference, suggested that researchers were fooling themselves over how well their apes were communicating. James Randi, a magician who spoke at the conference, explained how magic tricks often work by pulling the audience's attention away from what is actually going on. He added that he believed this was the case with chimp communication researchers and felt that they were committing this same type of fraud.

Although this conference did not bode well for cognition researchers, their work did continue. At a TED talk given in 2013, Dr. Reiss conversed with the musician Peter Gabriel; a computer engineer, Neil Gershenfeld; and one of the pioneers of the Internet, Vint Cerf. They presented the radical idea of a new internet that would help connect humans to all intelligent animals, including apes, dolphins, and elephants.

Dr. Reiss had developed an underwater keyboard in the 1980s to use in her dolphin studies. It was a custom-made touchscreen, an ancestor of many portable devices you work on today. She wanted to offer the dolphins choice and control. The dolphins could tap particular keys for certain things, the computer would make a whistle sound, and the dolphin would get an object or an activity. This gave the dolphins the ability to ask for a toy, such as a ball.

The dolphins were able to explore this keyboard on their own, similar to how we would work without an instruction manual. They played with the keyboard and tested it. Soon they figured out how it worked. They learned this on their own—an example of self-organized learning. Pretty cool!

How does that translate to something called an Interspecies Internet? Dr. Reiss received a call from Peter Gabriel. He knew musicians from all around the world who don't speak the same language, but when they played together, music became the common language they shared.

Gabriel told her about an amazing music-making experience. It wasn't with a famous musician, or even a human musician; it was with Kanzi's bonobo sister Panbanisha. He had contacted the primatologist Sue Savage-Rumbaugh, who worked with the bonobo, and was able to sit down with Panbanisha at a keyboard. At first the bonobo banged on the keys just like a small child would; then she was directed to use only one finger. Savage-Rumbaugh asked Panbanisha to play a quiet grooming song. Gabriel jammed behind her on his own keyboard while Savage-Rumbaugh encouraged her. What developed was a hauntingly beautiful, simple grooming song they created together.

Gabriel recounts what followed: "So that night, we began to dream, and we thought, perhaps the most amazing tool that man's created is the Internet, and what would happen if we could somehow find new interfaces, visual-audio interfaces that would allow these remarkable sentient beings that we share the planet with access?" Gabriel had become curious about ani-

A view of the sheet of carefully designed lexigrams that the bonobos carry around with them.

mals, their ability to communicate, and what they thought. Could they communicate with us and with each other via the Internet?

The Internet was created more than thirty years ago, in the 1980s. The Interspecies Internet is a new idea that includes other species. As the Internet becomes one of the main ways humans communicate with our appliances and other devices, we are also learning how to interface with things that are not human. This leaves lots of possibilities for communication with other species. "All kinds of possible sentient beings may be interconnected through this system, and I can't wait to see these experiments unfold," claims Cerf.

The Interspecies Internet is not a reality yet, but it is in progress. Researchers around the world are working on making this idea a reality.

One project, Apps4Apes, is centered on giving orangutans iPads for enrichment. Sponsored by Orangutan Outreach, the project aims to give apes access to music, instruments, cognitive games, art, and videos. A number of

SMITHSONIAN'S NATIONAL ZOO THINK TANK

Bonnie arrived at the National Zoo in 1980. The beautiful, large orangutan with the dark red coat has been a regular visitor to the Think Tank since the Zoo's O Line was introduced in 1994 to enable the apes to move freely between the Great Ape House and the Think Tank.

Unlike her fellow apes, Bonnie chooses to walk on two feet, like her human researchers, instead of four.

I must have been one of the first visitors to the Think Tank when it opened in the 1990s. It was mesmerizing to watch the orangs in action at touchscreens. Bonnie has been there the entire time, entrancing visitors and her keepers with her skills and intellect.

Another cool thing about Bonnie is that she can whistle, something even I can't do! It's a first for an orangutan and demonstrates that some apes can learn vocalizations from other species. Way to go, Bonnie!

Known to some as "Brainy Bonnie," this orangutan has made a name for herself at the National Zoo for her keen intelligence and charisma.

Many zoos, like the National Zoo, work hard to provide their animals with activities that will enhance their lives and enable us to learn from them.

zoos are already involved. Researchers at the Smithsonian's National Zoo are helping orangutans get stimulation by enabling them to use painting and keyboard apps on iPads.

New apps are continually added to give the orangutans choices. Thirty-two-year-old Bonnie, for example, likes the drums, but Kyle prefers the piano keyboard. Another often chooses to look at an app that shows fish swimming. These computers are given to them as long as they are interested.

The importance of communication cannot be overestimated in any species. Through communication, animals are able to locate food, avoid enemies, find mates, and care for their young. Humans are compulsive communicators. Just look at how many ways we reach out to each other. We talk. We write. We create art. And we now use many devices. Wouldn't it be something to one day find ourselves communicating with an orangutan on our iPads?

Beau is one of the dolphins living and being studied at the National Aquarium.

SELF-AWARENESS
MIRROR, MIRROR

Visitors pack the stands at the National Aquarium in Baltimore, Maryland, eager to see the dolphins perform. Beau, one of eight Atlantic bottlenose dolphins living there, swims inside the large saltwater tank. Outside the tank stands a dolphin specialist, Kerry Diehl. Kerry holds a mirror up to the side of the tank. Beau swims over to the side and gives a look through the glass to the shiny surface on the other side.

What do you see when you look in a mirror? Is it some wild-eyed stranger looking back at you, or your own familiar face? Humans are what scientists call self-aware. We recognize the face in the mirror as our own. But do animals recognize themselves when they see their reflection in a mirror or in

Human babies transition to toddler stage with three important abilities: language, mobility, and self-awareness. Although some scientists believe self-awareness might happen a little earlier, most follow the studies that indicate that human babies will begin looking into a mirror and recognizing their reflection between one and three years old. The same mirror tests have been conducted on babies by placing a mark of red makeup on their face. Younger infants point to the mirror, but as they get older, they touch the mark on their face when they look in the mirror.

water? Does Beau see himself, or does he think the face in the mirror is another dolphin?

Research has shown that humans are not the only animals who possess this trait of self-awareness. Apes do, which isn't too surprising since they are so closely related to us, but they aren't alone. Dolphins and elephants have now joined the list.

Dr. Diana Reiss, author of *Dolphin in the Mirror,* has been studying dolphins for years. Her first study lab was at Marine World in California, but these days she spends most of her time studying the dolphins at the National Aquarium in Baltimore. Her laboratory is a glass booth in the dolphin pool.

"I climb into it with a video camera. The animals are used to me," says Dr. Reiss.

As mentioned earlier, dolphins have very large brains relative to their body size, second only to humans. Scientists refer to this measurement as

Dolphins may look like fish, but they are mammals with behaviors that more closely resemble those of elephants and primates. There are thirty species of marine dolphins, including orca whales, the largest member of the dolphin family. Dolphins have been observed using tools, working in teams to catch fish, and can recognize the individual whistles of other dolphins years after they've seen each other. Beau is just one of the aquarium's dolphins that were born in captivity. He has never been in the wild, and scientists believe it would risk his life to release him.

the encephalization quotient. This means dolphins have the capability to be very smart. We've seen how they have complex communication skills and have the potential for communicating with us. But do they recognize themselves when they look in a mirror? Reiss wanted to find out.

Gordon Gallup, a psychologist who created the mirror self-recognition test in 1970 while shaving in front of a mirror, told Reiss about his experiences using the test with chimpanzees. Gallup had been inspired to create the test by an account of Charles Darwin's visit to the London Zoo in 1838. When Darwin visited the zoo he was impressed with an orangutan named Jenny. Jenny acted human-like during the visit and had been drawing crowds to her enclosure. Darwin wrote to his sister that Jenny was "astonished beyond measure" by her reflection in a mirror. This small mention in a letter written over one hundred years earlier drew Gallup's attention. He recognized the significance and devised the experiment that became known as the mirror test. Together, he and Reiss decided to test the dolphins.

"Most animals—if they do pay attention to a mirror, which many don't, like dogs and cats generally don't—they think it's another of their own kind, and they'll show social behavior. With the dolphins, not only are they aware that it's themselves, they show it to us behaviorally," says Reiss.

When Reiss put a mirror in the dolphin tank at the aquarium she found that the first thing they did was to look over it and behind it. They whistle or squawk to reach out to it socially. Then they do something called *contingency testing*. Reiss describes it as a series of imitations, like a fun mirror game you might play at camp. The dolphins do something in front of the mirror and then study the reflection.

"So, what they do is they'll look inside their mouths, and they'll open their mouths really wide," says Reiss. "Dolphins will often wiggle their tongues."

These behaviors all indicate self-awareness. They're the same behaviors we perform!

"They all put their eyes up against the mirror and look at their eyes very closely," says Reiss.

This was an important discovery. We used to think that humans from the age of two on were the only animals who could recognize their faces in a mirror. We now know that apes and dolphins also have the ability. This demonstrates that dolphins think. They can differentiate themselves from other individuals. They know the concepts of "self" and "others."

Dr. Diana Reiss was the scientific advisor on the 2009 documentary film *The Cove*, which dealt with dolphin slaughter. At the time, few scientists were speaking out about this practice. She was so upset about these deaths that she got a group of biologists and aquarium professionals together to form a dolphin conservation organization, Act for Dolphins. "My feeling is if we can't stop thirty-four fishermen from treating these animals so miserably, then what hope is there for fixing anything in this world. One reason I study dolphins is that I believe that knowing about them is one step in saving them."

Beau takes a look in the mirror and sees himself.

"And it helps us understand that humans share higher thinking abilities with some other animals," says Reiss.

Beau sees himself inside the shiny surface of the mirror. He knows he's not looking at another dolphin. After Reiss's experiments, the staff, including Kerry, began using the mirror as a regular part of the dolphin's enrichment activities. Beau plays with the mirror just as he plays with his other toys in the tank.

After her experiments with dolphins, Dr. Reiss moved on to study elephants. They have large brains also. Reiss joined Frans de Waal and one of his graduate students, Josh Plotnick, in an experiment to see if elephants would do the same thing. Years before, a mirror had been put on the ground outside the enclosure of a captive elephant and the experiment failed: the elephants did not show any signs of recognition.

Why do you think the experiment failed? The elephant could see only its legs behind the bars of its enclosure. It could not see itself well enough to examine the mirror properly or move any parts of its body to see them in the mirror. Despite these obvious flaws in the experiment design, those early researchers determined that the elephant lacked self-awareness.

But that was a long time ago. When Plotnick and the team repeated the experiment at the Bronx Zoo in New York City in 2006, they made one very big change. They enabled the elephants—Maxine, Patty, and Happy—to see, smell, and touch an eight-foot-square mirror. The mirror was constructed of plastic rather than glass, making it safer for the large animals, especially if they were to touch it with their trunks or feet. It was framed in steel and bolted to a wall.

Not only did the Asian elephants recognize themselves, they were able to touch themselves. Happy continually rubbed a painted mark on her forehead, which she could have performed only if she connected the image in the mirror to her own elephant body. She didn't rub the image on the mirror; she rubbed her forehead. When the story about these elephants broke in 2006, the AP ran a story with the appropriate opening line, "If you're Happy and you know it, pat your head."

Most animals will look at their reflection and believe it to be a stranger, which they will attempt to greet. These elephants waved their trunks at their reflection and moved their heads in and out of view, just like a human would do.

Elephants, like this Asian elephant, also have the ability to recognize themselves in the mirror.

These mirror studies were conducted on captive animals, but Reiss mentioned in her TED talk that self-awareness has also been found recently in magpies in the wild. It seems that magpies might not be so bird brained after all!

Dr. Helmut Prior at Goethe University in Frankfurt, Germany, stuck yellow and red dots on the necks of five magpies. A mirror was placed in front of the birds for half of the experiment. A nonreflective plate was placed in front of them in the other half of the trials.

Asian elephants are giant herbivores, standing up to ten feet tall and weighing up to 11,000 pounds. They use their trunk and their teeth to gather and eat lots of plants, including leaves, bark, grasses, and crops. At the National Zoo, elephants eat 125 pounds of hay, ten pounds of food pellets, ten pounds of vegetables and fruits, and some leafy tree branches each day. They are listed as endangered in the wild due to hunting and habitat loss. They have the largest brain of any land mammal and communicate with moans, bellows, rumbles, and low-frequency sounds that are too low for human ears. Frans de Waal's graduate assistant, Joshua Plotnick, became hooked on trying to save these intelligent creatures. In 2007 he traveled to Asia and by 2011 had founded Think Elephants to work on conservation by educating children about elephant behavior.

The birds could not see the dots without looking in the mirror. The researchers found that the birds scratched at their necks after seeing themselves in a mirror with the dots. The researchers also experimented with a black dot, which blended in with the black feathers of the magpies. The birds with those stickers didn't scratch at their necks. They also did not scratch their necks in front of the nonreflective surface, indicating that they didn't see the black dot against their black feathers.

Like the dolphins and the elephants, two of the magpies also repeatedly looked behind the mirror, indicating contingency testing.

Dr. Frans de Waal points out that magpies' brains are large in relation to their body size. Not all birds have big brains, nor do they exhibit the same behavior. This research demonstrates that magpies can recognize themselves—the first time this has been shown in a nonmammal.

Prior and his colleagues believe that self-awareness in mammals and birds may be a situation of convergent evolution. This means that each species experienced similar pressures as it was evolving and reached the same traits and behaviors through different paths.

MENTAL TIME TRAVEL
DOG DREAMS

Your dog is stretched out in the sun fast asleep with his tail wagging. He must be dreaming about the cat he chased the day before, right? Not so, says Dr. Ira Hyman, professor of psychology at Western Washington University.

Hyman claims, "Dogs don't remember what happened yesterday and don't plan for tomorrow."

Chronesthesia, or mental time travel, is the ability to understand that yesterday is different from today and that tomorrow will also be different. Dr. Hyman defines *episodic remembering* as the "combination of a self concept and mental time travel; recollecting the self in that other time period." It's like when you remember yourself sitting at your classroom desk last year. You can picture yourself at the desk and remember what was going on around you.

"First, in order to experience episodic remembering, an individual must have a sense of self. Most non-human animals have a dramatically different experience of self than we do. For example, most animals (and young humans) fail to identify themselves in mirrors," says Dr. Hyman.

Being able to mentally time travel to the past also enables the ability to plan for the future, a trait that sets humans apart from other animals. We save money for our first car, for college, and even retirement and can see that our future will be different from our present.

Dogs have a host of talents, but remembering the past or planning for tomorrow isn't one of them.

Dogs can't plan for events, although they do have expectations. They expect when they will be fed, but they don't plan for it. It has been thought that all animals are stuck in the present and don't have this ability.

Does this mean that dogs are stuck in the ever-present? Are they the true embodiment of living for today? Perhaps.

But Charles Darwin and Dr. Mark Bekoff, a former professor of ecology and evolutionary biology at the University of Colorado, have different points of view. Darwin imagined that dogs do indeed reflect on the past. Bekoff points to many examples of dogs who "remember"—dogs who have been abused and continually exhibit fear for years, dogs who remember where they've hid things, and dogs who change their behavior based on what they've learned.

"There's no evidence that dogs are stuck in an 'eternal present.' So, all in all, unless others and I are missing something, dogs do remember yesterday," counters Bekoff.

Dogs may indeed remember, but the question remains if they can project and plan for the future.

The Western scrub jay (*Aphelocoma californica*) is a member of the crow (Corvid) family, a relative of the magpie, a songbird in the same family. It is native to western North America. Corvids and primates split into two different evolutionary paths about 300 million years ago.

While researchers are debating whether dogs exhibit the ability to mentally time travel, scientists have accepted that a member of the crow family, the Western scrub jay, has demonstrated future thinking.

BIRD BRAINS

Dr. Arii Watanabe of the University of Cambridge in the United Kingdom devised an experiment. He allowed five scrub jays to watch as two researchers hid a yummy waxworm (a caterpillar larva of the wax moth). The first researcher had a choice of hiding the worm in any of four open cups in front of him. The other researcher had three covered cups and one open one. The worms could only be placed in an open, uncovered cup. Both researchers hid the food at the same time. The birds had to choose which researcher to watch.

They hypothesized that the jays should realize that they could find the second researcher's food easily. The worm had to be in the open cup. This should lead the birds to watch the first researcher, because witnessing the setup of the cups and the placement of the worm would be more useful to them in the future.

After conducting the experiment, the researchers found that the birds did indeed watch the first researcher. They did exhibit future thinking! This is a great discovery. It provides further evidence that we are not the only species that thinks about thinking. Watanabe says it best: "Some birds study for a test like humans do."

Dr. Nicola Clayton of the University of Cambridge also conducted an experiment to find out if scrub jays plan for the future. In one experiment the jays were able to stay in a compartment with peanuts or one with dog kibble on alternate mornings. After several days the jays were able to travel between the two compartments. Would the jays plan for the future and hoard some food for later?

The time-traveling jays did plan ahead. They buried peanuts in the compartment that held the kibble and buried kibble in the compartment that held the peanuts. No matter which compartment they were housed in, they were guaranteed they wouldn't have a shortage of food.

WAIT FOR IT . . .

If you ever pay attention to commercials, you might think that humans have no willpower at all and that we are helpless when tempted by the newest shiny car or the biggest dessert. But actually, we do have the power to be goal-directed. We can delay what we want in order to get something better in the future. We can exhibit patience. So can other primates, at least for a short time. They can wait for a few minutes if they have the opportunity to get a better reward later.

Let's look at another experiment with birds. It's commonly thought that animals always give in to their immediate needs. And science has shown that many animals, such as chickens and rats, have a difficult time delaying a food reward over one that they can have immediately. But they aren't brainy crows. Corvids have big brains and have exhibited complex thinking, as we've seen with scrub jays and magpies. Let's see if they can also show a little patience.

Dr. Valerie Dufour of the University of Strasbourg in France has found that crows and ravens can wait for more than five minutes if they believe they will obtain a better reward. That's the same as primates. They even employ activities to distract themselves from waiting, just like we do.

Dufour studied six ravens and six crows. The birds were trained to exchange tokens for food rewards. After they accomplished that task, they were tested on delaying the exchange. The researcher would hand a bird a piece of food, which it could eat immediately. After a specified waiting time the researcher would give a signal and the bird could exchange the piece for an even more desirable food reward if it hadn't already eaten the first one.

The bird would obtain the new reward only if it waited the entire time period without eating the original piece. If it tried to exchange the piece too early, it wouldn't receive the new reward either. The birds showed that they

Being called a bird brain would be a compliment if you were being compared to a crow.

could wait for a better reward, but as the time of the wait increased, they had more difficulty.

The longer the birds had to wait, the more likely they were to deposit the original piece in a crack, similar to the out-of-sight-out-of-mind technique of waiting. You may do that at home with your snacks. Along with their other cognitive skills, corvids can make some judgment about the future.

THE SPOON TEST

A group of researchers at the Primatology Centre of the University of Strasbourg conducted an experiment with brown capuchin and Tonkean macaque monkeys to test their future thinking abilities. Most animals are unable to act in the present to alleviate future hunger or thirst.

The researchers based their experiment on the cognitive scientist Endel

Endel Tulving used an Estonian children's story to describe his spoon test: "A young girl dreams about going to a friend's birthday party where the guests are served delicious chocolate pudding, her favorite. Alas, all she can do is to watch other children eat it, because everybody has to have her own spoon, and she did not bring one. So the next evening, determined not to have the same disappointing experience again, she goes to bed clutching a spoon in her hand."

This example has become the best test of mental time travel. Scientists use the spoon test as a basis to design experiments for both young children and nonhuman animals.

Tulving's 2005 spoon test in which he describes a girl who wanted to eat pudding at a party but had no spoon. When faced with another party, would she think ahead and bring her own spoon? Tulving had the view that humans were alone in their ability to have episodic memory. His spoon test demonstrates that this girl is able to reflect on her party experience and to project the possibility of another party.

In their version of the spoon test, the researchers set up a situation allowing monkeys to exchange a token for a food reward at a set time during the day. The monkeys would get used to this activity, making it predictable. The researchers then gave the monkeys a time when they could collect tokens in advance of the exchange. The monkeys would have to collect the tokens and save them until the time to exchange them for food. If they failed to collect and transport the tokens to the exchange, they wouldn't get any food. Like the little girl who needed to bring along a utensil to eat, the monkeys would have to remember that they would need tokens the next day to receive food.

The monkeys mostly failed to transport the tokens when entering the testing compartment for the exchange. This led researchers to the conclusion that they lacked the ability to plan for the future.

Can the great apes perform better? Yes. Again using Tulving's spoon test as a model, researchers Nicholas Mulcahy and Josep Call found that bonobos and orangutans would select, transport, and save tools for later use. They concluded that the precursor skills for future planning evolved in great

Nyota, like the other bonobos at Ape Cognition and Conservation Initiative, carries his lexigram chart to communicate with the human researchers.

apes more than 14 million years ago, when all great apes shared a common ancestor.

Humans have the ability to mentally time travel into the future even if we can't physically achieve it. Scientists believe that this trait evolved along with us and provided our species with an edge over other animals.

"Without it, there would be no planning, no building, no culture; without an imagined picture of the future, our civilization would not exist," wrote Dan Falk in *In Search of Time: The History, Physics, and Philosophy of Time.*

It must certainly give an edge to any species that possesses even a trace of it, even the crow cawing away in your backyard.

Bonobos share 98.5 percent of our DNA and possess many human-like traits. They have the ability in captivity to pick up many facets of human culture just from observation. Bonobos have been observed using paintbrushes, making music, and cooking. They live in the wild in the forests of the Democratic Republic of Congo, where their status is endangered. Civil war has greatly impacted their population by fragmenting them into isolated areas, which has limited their genetic diversity. Poverty has also forced people to kill bonobos for their meat and sell it on the black market.

Kandula, one of the elephant subjects of a study on animal cognition, has shown unparalleled problem-solving skills.

PROBLEM SOLVING
GOOD MORNING, KANDULA!

Kandula, a male Asian elephant, sees me across his enclosure at the Smithsonian National Zoo. It's early, and quite possibly I am the first visitor he's seen today. Two fences separate us, but he comes as close as he can and tips up a rubber tire toward me. I can't help but wonder if he wants to play.

I've come to the zoo today to check out this particular elephant, knowing that Dr. Diana Reiss learned something remarkable about him.

TOOL-USING ELEPHANTS

Dr. Reiss not only found that elephants are self-aware, but also did research into their problem-solving skills. Elephants had failed to exhibit anything insightful in previous studies. But Reiss and her team wanted to test three Asian elephants at the Smithsonian National Zoo to see if they would use sticks or other objects to get out-of-reach food. The elephant group consisted of two females, one thirty-three years old, the other sixty-one, and a seven-year-old male, Kandula.

None of the elephants used the bamboo sticks the researchers supplied to reach the food, although they did hold the sticks in their trunks and used them to scratch themselves, pry open doors, and hit the floors, walls, and hanging toys. It is unclear why they didn't use them to reach their food.

However, the researchers did observe Kandula moving a large plastic cube so that he could stand on it and reach a piece of hanging fruit. When the cube wasn't available, he stacked smaller objects to enable him to reach the food.

The team concluded that there was enough evidence to suggest that elephants are capable of problem solving using tools. Although elephants had previously been observed in other situations standing on objects to reach food, Kandula's movement of the cube indicated a higher level of thinking: he thought about how he could reach the food and then solved his problem by creating a tool to accomplish the task.

Other animals have used tools in more complex fashions. Have you ever tried to figure out how to open a puzzle box? It takes a lot of brainpower and patience. Now imagine a bird trying to solve a puzzle that complicated.

Kandula, having turned fourteen years old, is now at home at the Oklahoma City Zoo and Botanical Garden meeting new elephants to whom he is not related.

CLEVER CROWS

Dr. Alex Taylor, a lecturer at New Zealand's University of Auckland, conducted an experiment with a male New Caledonian crow named 007. He arranged three boxes and other objects in 007's enclosure. The crow had to complete eight steps using these objects to obtain the desired food reward. The crow had seen the steps before, but never in this order. The eight steps had to be completed in sequence for the bird to receive the food reward.

The crow hopped around from box to object, examining everything. Once he had a good look at everything, he began by pulling up a string that had a short stick tied to it. The crow took the stick into his beak, completing step one.

Dr. Taylor holding a New Caledonian Crow before its release.

The bird attempted to reach the food in one of the objects with the stick and found it to be too short. Next, he took the stick over to one of the boxes. The box was open on the side, with tiny wooden bars. Inside was a stone. The crow poked the stick through the bars to move the stone out between the bars. Step two was completed.

He dropped the stone onto the table and moved over to get another stone from the second box. He dropped that one on the table too. For a moment he seemed stumped; then he took one of the stones in his beak and dropped it into one of the other boxes. This action moved a lever down slightly. With each stone he put in, the lever moved down a little more. He repeated the steps: pick up stick, move stone, drop stone in box. The lever moved farther down. Soon the crow was up to the eighth step. The lever moved all the way down until it freed a longer stick. He then used the longer stick to free the food in the initial box. The New Caledonian crow, 007, solved the puzzle, got a reward, and lived up to his secret agent name!

New Caledonian crows are notorious problem solvers and tool users. They have even been shown to use tools to manipulate other tools—a trait normally seen only in humans and apes. But as we have seen, corvids have big brains and exhibit many remarkable behaviors.

Think about all of the tools—everything from a comb to a fork to a toothbrush—you use during the day. What skills or brainpower do you need to use them? To use tools, you need problem-solving skills, intelligence, and dexterity. Tools enable you to make your environment suit your needs instead of having to adapt to your environment. Tools should be to the user's advantage. They may help the user groom, obtain food, or build a home. Animals that use tools must have access to objects from which they can fashion tools—things like stones, wood, cactus spines, and shells. The crows of New Caledonia create tools out of all sorts of things, including their own feathers.

Aesop wrote a tale, "The Crow and the Pitcher," more than 2,500 years ago about a thirsty bird that was able to place stones in a pitcher to raise the level of water. Pliny the Elder also wrote about a crow doing this:

New Caledonian crows live on the islands of New Caledonia in the Pacific Ocean off the coast of Australia. Of medium size (as far as crows go) and all black, they are known for their tool-using skills. Scientists have also experimented with the birds' concept of causal agent. When a hidden causal agent (HCA) causes something to happen, we can't see the cause, but are able to recognize what it is. For example, if we hear thunder, we know that it was caused by a storm. Or if we see movement of leaves in a tree and there isn't any wind, we might guess that it was caused by a squirrel. When an unknown causal agent (UCA) causes something to happen, we don't know what the cause is. It's like the sound you might hear in your house that is unfamiliar and someone needs to check out. Although many animals, including macaques and chimpanzees, have been unable to make inferences even about HCAs, New Caledonian crows have been found to understand UCAs.

Primates have frequently been seen using tools.

A crow that was thirsty was seen heaping stones into the urn on a monument, in which there was some rain-water which it could not reach; and so, being afraid to go down to the water, by thus accumulating the stones, it caused as much water to come within its reach as was necessary to satisfy its thirst.

Thousands of years later scientists tested this behavior and found that, indeed, crows have that ability. But crows and elephants aren't the only animals using tools to solve their problems.

Otters smash their mollusks on rocks to get to the meat inside. An octopus will use a coconut shell as armor. Dolphins use marine sponges on their beaks to uncover prey on the ocean floor while protecting their delicate skin. They also have demonstrated cooperation in working together to pull the cap off a PVC pipe that researchers had filled with fish.

Apes have also demonstrated the use of tools. Gorillas have been known to use branches to test the depth of water of a swamp they need to cross. Wild capuchin monkeys crack open nuts with stones, just like humans would. My bonobo friend Kanzi can be seen on YouTube creating a campfire by gathering wood and using a lighter to start the fire. Although Kanzi's tool use is not spontaneous or wild, it is still quite extraordinary.

Scientists are constantly observing more and more uses of tools among animals. Although using tools is somewhat common, constructing tools is not. That requires higher cognitive skills.

FROM THINKING ANIMALS TO PROTECTED ANIMALS
OUR FELLOW CREATURES

Now that we know that rats exhibit empathy, that dolphins recognize themselves in a mirror, and that monkeys forgive each other, how can anyone still consider animals to be machines or robots?

The issue is no longer accepting that animals think; it's now the challenge of figuring out *how* they think and what we will do with that information.

John Pilley, author of *Chaser: Unlocking the Genius of the Dog Who Knows a Thousand Words,* agrees: "It is past time to abandon Descartes' paradigm of animals as machines and replace it with a paradigm of animals as truly our fellow creatures—biologically, emotionally, and cognitively—and of humans as wholly a part of nature."

Animal cognition scientists are discovering more and more with each study. Dr. Laurie Santos's research suggests that primates are "reasoning about things they can't see and interpreting mental states," something that we didn't believe they could do. It is just one more example demonstrating that the mental lives of animals are far richer than we believed.

According to the primatologist Frans de Waal, the scientists studying animal cognition these days have transformed Aristotle's ladder of nature "into a bush with many branches."

The more we find out about animals, the more we learn that they exhibit many processes that connect them to each other and to us.

"With every passing year the cognitive gap that supposedly differentiates us from mere animals is shrinking," says Dr. Nicholas Dodman, a professor at Cummings School of Veterinary Medicine at Tufts University and founder of Tufts' Animal Behavior Clinic. As this gap decreases, humans continue to wrestle with how we treat animals. The more we learn about how their minds work and what they understand, the more important the way we treat them becomes.

We live in a world where dogs are employed to rescue us but, in some countries, they are still used for food. We know elephants mourn their dead, are self-aware, and suffer depression, and yet they are slaughtered for their tusks and continue to be enslaved in circuses.

Fortunately, the history of animal welfare is older than the acceptance of the belief that animals can think. Saint Francis of Assisi, an Italian Catholic friar and preacher, said, "Not to hurt our humble brethren [the animals] is our first duty to them, but to stop there is not enough. We have a higher mission—to be of service to them whenever they require it . . ."

Henry Bergh founded the American Society for the Prevention of Cruelty to Animals (ASPCA) 150 years ago, in 1866. It still is one of the most powerful voices in animal protection.

Thomas Edison said, "Until we stop harming all living beings, we are still savages."

And Temple Grandin has been an outspoken advocate for animals that we breed for food, as well as our pets.

The Nonhuman Rights Project, founded in 2007 by an attorney, Steven Wise, has taken animal rights to another level. It is the only civil rights organization in the United States striving to achieve legal rights for animals other than humans. Its mission is to change the legal status of certain cognitively complex nonhuman animals, such as chimpanzees, elephants, dolphins, and whales, from "things" to "persons." As "persons" these animals would possess fundamental rights, including the right to *habeas corpus*. Habeas corpus is the right to seek relief from unlawful imprisonment.

These specific nonhuman animals have been selected for this protection because research has shown that they use sophisticated communication, solve difficult problems, mourn the loss of their loved ones, exhibit deep emotions, and live in complicated societies. The Nonhuman Rights Project's first cases were filed in 2013 on behalf of captive chimpanzees.

Even with all of these advocates and organizations, there is still much that needs to be changed. Fortunately, we all have the ability to make a difference.

We can observe.

We can study.

We can learn.

And most of all, we can protect.

THE NONHUMAN RIGHTS PROJECT STAFF SELECT THEIR PLAINTIFFS USING THREE CRITERIA:

1. They look at the bedrock qualities, such as the cognitive abilities observed by Dr. Jane Goodall (who is on the organization's board of directors), that courts value when determining whether an individual is a "legal person" who should possess certain fundamental rights.

2. They examine the relevant decisions and statutes of every state and how they might affect a court's ruling.

3. They search for highly cognitive animals who may reside in those states that are most favorable.

Behind an assortment of trailers in a cluttered lot in upstate New York is an aluminum-sided shed. Inside the small door is a small green metal animal cage containing some plastic toys, a small portable television, and a chimpanzee named Tommy. He is one of the plaintiffs the Nonhuman Rights Project has taken on. Tommy, who is around twenty-seven years old, spends his days inside this enclosure, but also has access to an outside playground jungle gym. Steven Wise visited the site and seven weeks later filed papers in the Fulton County Courthouse to bring a landmark case to court. Tommy would be the first nonhuman primate to sue his captor for unlawfully imprisoning him.

It isn't unusual for an animal to be in court. In the Middle Ages animals were often brought up on charges that extended from disrupting church services to murder. Those courtroom scenes were complete with lawyers and some stiff penalties. More recently animal welfare and endangered species cases have been brought before our court system.

In December 2014 a New York State appeals court deemed Tommy "property" and not a person. The five-judge panel concluded that because Tommy, as a chimpanzee, cannot be held responsible for his actions or cannot bear legal duties, he is not entitled to habeas corpus.

Can animals have rights? They sure can. But can they have the same rights as humans? That's what the Nonhuman Rights Project is trying to establish for highly cognitive animals, like Tommy, who spends his life in a small enclosure.

You might not think your cat is as smart as your dog, but its brain is a little more complex. Actually, a cat has about double the number of nerve cells in its cerebral cortex that a dog has.

AFTERWORD— ON CATS

Have you noticed that no cats are mentioned in this book? As a proud cat owner, I'd be remiss not to say something about their omission. It's not because cats aren't smart; they are. But there is not much research on cat cognition. Maybe you'll take that on yourself!

In March 1876 an interesting article ran in the *New York Times* about employing postal cats. The article questioned why no one had made an effort to develop the intellectual powers of domestic cats for the benefit of humans. It went on to profess the attributes of cats and how they are misunderstood.

Those who are intimately acquainted with the domestic cat must sometimes wonder why no effort has been made to develop his intellectual powers. There is no doubt that the cat possesses a strong and subtle intellect, and the capacity to use it for the benefit of mankind. And yet this able beast is currently believed to waste his vast abilities in the frivolous pleasures of the chase, or in more questionable forms of dissipation. No animal has been more thoroughly misunderstood by the careless and prejudiced observers who constitute the majority of mankind. Because the cat is a beast of refined tastes, accustomed to wear neat and elegant fur, and preferring to sleep on cushions rather than door-mats, he has been constantly classed among useless and brainless dandies.

In answer to this, it was recommended by the Belgian Society for the Elevation of the Domestic Cat that cats be used to transport mail. The village of Liège actually trained thirty-seven postal cats to deliver mail!

In the same article direction was given as to how the cats would carry the mail.

Messages are to be fastened in water-proof bags around the necks of the animals, and it is believed that, unless the criminal class of dogs undertakes to waylay and rob the mail-cats, the messages will be delivered with rapidity and safety.

The postal cats were not successful—much to the relief of postal workers all over the world!

Cats have been found to have better short-term memory than dogs.

INQUIRING MINDS WANT TO KNOW

You can study animals wherever you live. Whether you observe pigeon behavior outside your brownstone, squirrels in a local park, deer in your backyard, or your own dog, you can make exciting discoveries.

Record your observations.

FOLLOW THE STEPS

Take your research seriously and have fun while you do it! Use the scientific method to conduct your research. Record your activities in a notebook or on your computer. Here is a worksheet to follow:

1. Make an observation. Be curious! Be skeptical. Write down what you observe.
2. Develop a question. Identify a problem.
3. What are your goals? Make a plan.
4. Experiment to test your hypothesis. Gather evidence. Look at previous research.
5. Perform data analysis. Evaluate your evidence.
6. Write down your hypothesis.
7. Challenge your hypothesis with an experiment.
8. Develop a conclusion. What did you learn?

OBSERVE NATURALLY

Take Dr. Reiss's advice to her students and don't take any paper and pencil with you outside. Spend time just sitting and watching with no pressure to record. Afterward, write up the things you saw.

GET YOUR PET INVOLVED

If you own a pet, you have a unique opportunity to conduct your own animal cognition studies or help researchers with theirs. Here are a few things that you can do with your pet.

Canine Cognition Center at Yale: Help researchers find out what dogs are thinking. If you live in Connecticut, you can sign up your dog to take part in their canine research studies. It's no work and all play. Sign up at doglab.yale.edu.

C-BARQ: Register and fill out a canine behavioral assessment and research questionnaire at vetapps.vet.upenn.edu to help researchers at the University of Pennsylvania.

Dognition: You can share information about your dog's behavior with researchers through the Dognition program. There are twenty games that you can play with your dog at home. Instructions and videos are online at dognition.com. After you log in the data about your dog, you will receive a profile of your dog's cognition. Membership in the program is required.

Family Dog Project: Check out Familydogproject.elte.hu for the current projects.

Pets Can Do: By observing your cat or dog and filling out a survey, you can help University of Lincoln researchers. Visit Lincolnpetscando.uk.

DEVELOP YOUR OWN ANIMAL STUDY

You can set up your own animal study. Here is an example to get you started. This experiment was carried out by the Family Dog Project to explore a dog's guilty look. Try it at home with your own dog. Use the scientific method worksheet (the eight steps listed above) to organize your research.

Have you ever seen your dog look guilty when he's done something wrong? Maybe he has ripped up a toilet paper roll or chewed your homework. What does the dog do to look guilty? What do you observe?

Set up a study to find out if your dog is really feeling guilty or if there is another reason for that look. First, form a hypothesis in response to your question.

Next, conduct your experiment. Start by instructing your dog not to eat food off the table. Let your dog see you eat food at the table. Feed your dog separately. Take the food away or reprimand the dog if it tries to eat from the table. Repeat the behavior several times so that your dog learns not to eat food from the table.

Leave food on the table and leave the room. When you return, observe how your dog greets you. Does it exhibit any "guilty" behaviors? Greet the dog as usual and then go in and check the table. Did your dog eat the food you left behind? Record your observations in a journal.

Try the experiment with your friends' dogs. Did they exhibit the same behavior?

Read about the results of the guilty dog experiment in *The Dodo*:

www.thedodo.com/community/JulieHecht/does-your-dog-really-have-a
-gu-394593941.html and in *Scientific American*: blogs.scientificamerican
.com/dog-spies/2015/04/20/the-guilty-looking-companion.

OBSERVING IN THE OUTDOORS

Niko Tinbergen, one of the founders of the study of animal behavior and an
advocate of observing animals in the wild, wrote, "The curious naturalist
often feels sorry for those of his fellow-men who miss such an experience;
and miss it so unnecessarily, because it is there, to be seen, all the time."

Don't miss anything! Get out there and observe!

Project Squirrel: You can observe squirrels just about anywhere. Join
Project Squirrel, a great citizen science cognition project, at projectsquirrel
.org and begin sending your observations to scientists right away!

Get outside!

BECOME AN ANIMAL ADVOCATE

Many people believe they can raise our wild relatives in human settings. Chimpanzees are just one example. Lucy was a chimpanzee who was born in a U.S. circus. In 1964, Dr. Maurice K. Temerlin and his wife, Jane, took the chimp from her mother to raise in their home when she was just two days old. He wanted to know how "human" Lucy could become or if she would exhibit human emotions. They fed her with a bottle. By the time she was a year old she was eating at the table with her human parents. They dressed her in skirts and treated her like a human child. When she was about four or five years old they had someone teach her sign language.

Although Lucy did exhibit many human traits, including learning sign language, she was not meant to live in a human setting. Like all chimps, she grew very strong and it became too difficult to keep Lucy. Chimps will eventually outgrow their human homes. Although many states, counties, and towns have laws against owning nonhuman primates, many people still keep them as pets.

Join a group that advocates on their behalf, like the Jane Goodall Institute, or on behalf of other animals.

ORGANIZATIONS

Act for Dolphins—Join aquarium professionals, marine scientists, and Diana Reiss in working to protect dolphins. www.actfordolphins.org

The Alex Foundation—Inspired by Pepperberg's parrot, Alex, the Alex Foundation supports research that will expand the base of knowledge establishing the cognitive and communicative abilities of parrots as intelligent beings. alexfoundation.org

Ape Cognition and Conservation Initiative—Learn more about the bonobos of Iowa and how to conserve their species in the wild. apeinitiative.org

Apps for Apes—The Apps for Apes project is sponsored by Orangutan Outreach. See apes using iPads for enrichment and learn about ways that you can help. redapes.org/multimedia/apps-for-apes

Interspecies Internet—Learn more about the Interspecies Internet and watch videos of the research that is under way in animal communication. interspecies-internet.org

Jane Goodall Institute—You can help promote the work of Jane Goodall in protecting and preserving the population of apes and their habitat. www.janegoodall.org

The Nonhuman Rights Project—Read about the organization that is striving to give highly cognitive animals the rights of humans. www.nonhumanrightsproject.org

Think Elephants—Learn about elephant behavior, conservation, and research. thinkelephants.org

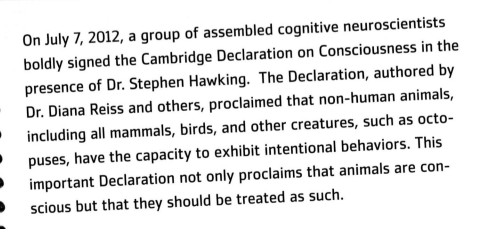

On July 7, 2012, a group of assembled cognitive neuroscientists boldly signed the Cambridge Declaration on Consciousness in the presence of Dr. Stephen Hawking. The Declaration, authored by Dr. Diana Reiss and others, proclaimed that non-human animals, including all mammals, birds, and other creatures, such as octopuses, have the capacity to exhibit intentional behaviors. This important Declaration not only proclaims that animals are conscious but that they should be treated as such.

WATCH AND LISTEN AND READ

Watch "What Are Animals Thinking" on *NOVA science NOW*:
www.youtube.com/watch?v=uoKQqVrVbeU

Watch 007, a problem-solving crow in action at:
www.youtube.com/watch?v=AVaITA7eBZE

Watch *The Dance of the Honeybee,* a Micro Challenge Final Film
from Peter Nelson:
vimeo.com/60000086
www.youtube.com/watch?v=AVaITA7eBZE

Watch Emory University's video that contrasts the portrayal of apes in
Planet of the Apes with real apes:
www.livescience.com/15451-chimps-humanlike-altruism.html

Watch the Cambridge Declaration being signed:
www.youtube.com/watch?v=W9QIOj3IYuk

READ:

Hesse, Karen. *The Music of Dolphins*. New York: Scholastic, 1998.

Montgomery, Sy. *The Octopus Scientists*. Boston: Houghton Mifflin
Harcourt, 2015.

Schrefer, Eliot. *Endangered*. New York: Scholastic, 2012.

ACKNOWLEDGMENTS

Writing books, especially nonfiction books, is like heading off on the yellow brick road. As you stroll on down, you meet exceptional people and have encounters that you may only have dreamed about. *Beastly Brains* was such a journey. I could not have begun it without my own good witch, my editor Erica Zappy Wainer, who allows me to have a voice and write books I am passionate about. Along the way I am grateful to so many, including Dr. Laurie Santos and Gisell Caraballo-Cruz for letting me tag along in Puerto Rico, even though I was hobbling along with a serious case of sciatica. Their patience was a blessing, and the island she shared with me was an experience I'll never forget. I also want to thank Natalie Castaldo, Kerry Diehl, and the dolphin team at the National Aquarium for such a great visit, and Scott Milne and the researchers at the Ape Cognition and Conservation Initiative for introducing me to Kanzi, Nyota, and my other bonobo friends. I am ever thankful to my writer buddies, family, and first readers, the team at Houghton Mifflin Harcourt, including designer extraordinaire Cara Llewellyn, and my amazing agent, Jennifer Laughran. Last, my endless love and gratitude go out to my camera assistant, wheelchair driver, and all-around travel buddy, my daughter, Lucie.

GLOSSARY

American Sign Language: a visual gesture language developed in the United States

anthropocentrism: the belief that humans are the most central and important species on the planet

anthropomorphism: attributing human characteristics to an animal or object

behaviorism: a school of psychology based on the belief that behaviors can be measured, trained, and changed

chronesthesia: the ability to be aware of one's past or future; also known as mental time travel

cognitive: relating to the activities of thinking, understanding, perception, learning, and reasoning

contingency testing: additional testing of a plan to see if the unexpected will happen

emotional contagion: the tendency for one individual to "catch" the emotion of another

empathy: the ability to understand and share the feelings of another

encephalization quotient: a measure of actual or predicted brain size for an animal of a known size, predicted to be an estimate of species intelligence or cognition

ethogram: a complete list of species-specific behaviors

ethology: the study of animal behavior, usually with a focus under natural environments

evolution: the gradual development of something from a simple to a more complex form

hive mind: a large number of people thinking and acting as a community, sharing knowledge and ideas

inequity aversion: a dislike for unfairness

innenwelt: inner world

instinct: natural impulse, something you don't need to learn

lexigram: a symbol that represents a word

operant conditioning: when a random response is positively rewarded to obtain the desired response

scala naturae: Latin concept for a chain of natural order, in which all living organisms fit in a linear hierarchy, from simple to complex

swarm intelligence: collective behavior of a group of animals, specifically social insects

TED talk: an eighteen-minute presentation from a TED (technology, entertainment, design) conference

umwelt: external world

SOURCE NOTES

PAGE

1. From Machine to Thinking Animal

7   "If we consider these several cases": Darwin, *The Formation of Vegetable Mould*, 40.

9   "What! that bird which makes": Voltaire, "Animals," in *The Philosophical Dictionary*, translated by H. J. Woolf (New York: Knopf, 1924); history.hanover.edu/texts/voltaire/volanima.html.

10   "It seems to me that they [worms]": Darwin, *The Life and Letters of Charles Darwin*, 419.

11   "various emotions and faculties": Darwin, *Descent of Man*, 106.
    Many a zoologist and physiologist: von Uexküll, "A Stroll Through the Worlds of Animals and Men," 5.

12   "Wondering what feelings or thoughts might motivate": Safina, "Big Love," 45.

13   "You cannot share your life": Quammen, "Jane: Fifty Years at Gombe," 120.

2. Entering the Lab

23   "For a scientist, knowing the questions to ask": Phone interview with Dr. Diana Reiss, March 2015.

25 "A question answered usually raises new problems": Karl von Frisch, "Decoding the Language of the Bee," in *Nobel Lectures, Physiology or Medicine 1971–1980,* ed. Jan Lindsten (Singapore: World Scientific Publishing, 1992), 86.

27 "Say a lion was stalking a zebra": Safina, "Big Love," 45.

28 "When someone says you can't attribute": Safina, "Big Love," 47.

29 "There are birds that see ultraviolet": Wynne, *Animal Cognition,* 18.

30 "We must first blow . . . a soap bubble around each creature": von Uexküll, "A Stroll Through the Worlds of Animals and Men," 5.

31 "Sometimes the monkeys just walk away": Interview with Dr. Laurie Santos, March 12, 2015.

3. Making Decisions

36 "Did he think the spot was beautiful": Marsa, "The 'Monkey Whisperer,'" 58.

37 "We pay too much attention to losses": Email from Dr. Laurie Santos to author, April 2015.

41 "But it was not known if these processes": Prigg, "Apes Are Sore Losers."

42 "If you see something in a primate": Adler, "Thinking Like a Monkey."

46 "The head butting serves": Phone interview with Dr. Thomas Seeley, October 30, 2015.

46   "Honeybee swarms and complex brains": Thomas Seeley at al., "Stop Signals Provide Cross Inhibition in Collective Decision-Making by Honeybee Swarms," *Science* 335, no. 6064 (January 6, 2012): 108–11.

4. Emotions and Empathy

55   "I am not even particularly interested": De Waal, *The Age of Empathy*, 131.

       "I think that the rat's mind": Twain, *What Is Man*, 76–77.

56   "biologically mandated": "What Are Animals Thinking?"

57   "The principle is that you have a valuable relationship": Dr. Frans de Waal, "Moral Behavior in Animals," TED Talk, April 2012.

59   "For me, the most important find": Choi, "Like Humans, Chimps Show Selfless Behaviors."

       "One is reciprocity": Dr. Frans de Waal, "Moral Behavior in Animals," TED Talk, April 2012.

5. Fairness

62   "Of jealousy in dogs innumerable instances might be given": Romanes, *Animal Intelligence*, 142.

63   "Such jealousy seems to me a very advanced emotion": Romanes, *Animal Intelligence*, 443.

       "If a master is not equal in his ways towards his dogs": Romanes, *Animal Intelligence*, 443.

64   "Don't necessarily have to have an idea of fairness": Palca, "Monkey Business."

6. Communication

72   "The question is not how smart are dolphins": Foer, "It's Time for a Conversation," 47.

75   "Long Before Koko, Nim, and Washoe were born": "Comparative Tests on a Chimpanzee and Human Infant, Part 1," www.youtube.com/watch?v=pwRgUKRA2iU.

81   "unprofessional, unpleasant attempt": Susan Fowler, "The Clever Hans Phenomenon Conference," *International Journal for the Study of Animal Problems* 1, no. 6 (1980): 355–59.

83   "All kinds of possible sentient beings may be interconnected": Vint Cerf, "Interspecies Internet?" TED Talk, February 2013.

7. Self-Awareness

89   "Most animals—if they do pay attention to a mirror": Ira Flatow, "A Researcher Asks: Are Dolphins Self-Aware?" *Talk of the Nation,* November 4, 2011.

8. Mental Time Travel

96   "Dogs don't remember what happened yesterday": Hyman, "Dogs Don't Remember."

96   "First, in order to experience episodic remembering": Hyman, "Dogs Don't Remember."

98   "There's no evidence that dogs are stuck": Bekoff, "Dogs Don't Remember Yesterday."

99   "Some birds study": Goldman, "Western Scrub Jays."

102   "A young girl dreams about": Tulving, "Episodic Memory and Autonoesis," 44.

105   "Without it, there would be no planning": Falk, *In Search of Time*, 105.

9. Problem Solving

113   "A crow that was thirsty": Pliny, *Natural History of Pliny*, 525–26.

10. From Thinking Animals to Protected Animals

114   "It is past time to abandon Descartes' paradigm": Pilley, "Descartes the Bogeyman."

      "into a bush with many branches": De Waal, "The Brains of the Animal Kingdom."

116   "With every passing year": Nicholas Dodman, "Animals Have Emotions, but What About 'Theory of Mind'?" *Veterinary Practice News*, September 30, 2013.

Afterword: On Cats

121   "Those who are intimately acquainted": "Postal Cats," *New York Times*, March 1876.

BIBLIOGRAPHY

Adler, Jerry. "Thinking Like a Monkey." *Smithsonian*, January 2008; www.smithsonianmag.com/science-nature/thinking-like-a -monkey-8265488.

Alcock, John. *Animal Behavior: An Evolutionary Approach*. Sunderland, Mass.: Sinauer Assoc., 1979.

Bekoff, Marc. "Dogs Don't Remember Yesterday, Claims Psychologist." *Psychology Today*, March 5, 2015; www.psychologytoday.com/blog/ animal-emotions/201503/dogs-dont-remember-yesterday-claims -psychologist.

———. "Animals Are Conscious and Should Be Treated As Such." *New Scientist*, no. 2283, September 22, 2012; www.newscientist.com/ article/mg21528836-200-animals-are-conscious-and-should-be -treated-as-such.

"A Bird's Eye View of Art." Psychology & Sociology, *Animal Cognition*, June 30, 2009.

Bourjade, Marie, et al. "Are Monkeys Able to Plan for Future Exchange?" *Animal Cognition* 15, no. 5 (2012): 783–95.

Boysen, Sarah. *The Smartest Animals on the Planet*. Buffalo, N.Y.: Firefly, 2009.

Braconnier, Deborah. "Parrots Display Teamwork and Decision-Making Skills." Phys.org, May 19, 2011.

Castaldo, Nancy. "Animal Communication." *Conservationist*, September/October 1992.

Choi, Charles Q. "Like Humans, Chimps Show Selfless Behaviors." *Live Science*, August 8, 2011; www.livescience.com/15451-chimps-humanlike-altruism.html.

Darwin, Charles. *The Descent of Man, and Selection in Relation to Sex.* Second ed. London, 1896.

———. *The Formation of Vegetable Mould Through the Action of Worms with Observations of Their Habits.* London: John Murray, Albemarle St., 1896.

De Waal, Frans. *The Age of Empathy.* New York: Harmony Books, 2009.

———. "The Brains of the Animal Kingdom." *Wall Street Journal*, March 22, 2013; www.wsj.com/articles/SB100014241278873238696045783705742853382756.

Dufour, V., et al. "Corvids Can Decide if a Future Exchange Is Worth Waiting For." *Biology Letters* 8, no. 2 (April 23, 2012).

Falk, Dan. *In Search of Time: The History, Physics, and Philosophy of Time.* New York: Thomas Dunne Books, 2008.

Feltman, Rachel. "New York Court Rules That Tommy the Chimp Is Not a 'Person.'" *Washington Post*, December 4, 2014; www.washingtonpost

.com/news/speaking-of-science/wp/2014/12/04/new-york-court
-rules-that-tommy-the-chimp-is-not-a-person.

Flombaum, Jonathan I., and Laurie R. Santos. "Rhesus Monkeys Attribute Perceptions to Others." *Current Biology* 15, no. 5 (2005): 447–52.

Foer, Joshua. "It's Time for a Conversation: Breaking the Communication Barrier Between Dolphins and Humans." *National Geographic*, May 2015, 30–55.

Foerder, P., et al. "Insightful Problem Solving in an Asian Elephant." *PLoS ONE* 6, no. 8 (2011).

Goldman, Jason G. "Western Scrub Jays Are Capable of Metacognition." *Scientific American*, September 1, 2014; www.scientificamerican.com/ article/western-scrub-jays-are-capable-of-metacognition.

Grandin, Temple, and Catherine Johnson. *Animals in Translation: Using the Mysteries of Autism to Decode Animal Behavior*. New York: Scribner, 2005.

Greenfieldboyce, Nell. "Dogs Understand Fairness, Get Jealous, Study Finds." *Research News Morning Edition*, NPR, December 9, 2008.

Horner, Victoria, et al. "How Do Apes Ape?" *Learning and Behavior*, 2004, 36–52.

Horner, Victoria, et al. "Spontaneous Prosocial Choice by Chimpanzees." *National Academy of Sciences* 108, no. 33 (2011): 13847–51.

Hyman, Ira. "Dogs Don't, but Maybe Chimps Remember." *Psychology Today*, May 7, 2010.

————. "Dogs Don't Remember." *Psychology Today*, May 1, 2010; www.
    psychologytoday.com/blog/animal-emotions/201503/
    dogs-dont-remember.

Imperial College London. "Bird Brain? Birds and Humans Have Similar
    Brain Wiring." *ScienceDaily*, July 17, 2013.

Jabr, Ferris. "Jailbreak Rat: Selfless Rodents Spring Their Pals and Share
    Their Sweets." *Scientific American*, December 8, 2011.

Kerr, Dara. "Vint Cerf Sees an 'Interspecies Internet' to Talk with Animals."
    CNET, February 28, 2013; www.cnet.com/news/vint-cert-sees-an
    -interspecies-internet-to-talk-with-animals.

Kight, Caitlin. "Human Perceptions of Animal Cognition." *Science 2.0*, May,
    4, 2012; www.science20.com/anthrophysis/human_perceptions
    _animal_cognition-89722.

Locker, Melissa. "Shock the Monkey! Peter Gabriel Wants an Interspecies
    Internet. TIME.com, October 16, 2014; newsfeed.time.com/2013/03/05
    /peter-gabriel-interspecies-internet.

Marsa, Linda. "The 'Monkey Whisperer' Learns the Secrets of Primate
    Economics." *Discover*, October 13, 2008.

Masson, Jeffrey Moussaieff, and Susan McCarthy. *When Elephants Weep: The
    Emotional Lives of Animals*. New York: Delacorte, 1995.

Morell, Virginia. "Animal Minds." *National Geographic*, March 2008.

————. *Animal Wise: The Thoughts and Emotions of Our Fellow Creatures*.
    New York: Crown, 2013.

Mulcahy, N. J., and Josep Call. "Apes Save Tools for Future Use." *Science* 312 (May 19, 2006): 1038–40; www.cogs.indiana.edu/spackled/ 2012readings/Science-2006-Mulcahy-1038-40.pdf.

Palca, Joe. "Monkey Business: Fairness Isn't Just a Human Trait." *All Things Considered*, NPR, August 16, 2010.

Pilley, John W. "Descartes the Bogeyman—and the Dog Who's Nailing His Coffin Shut." *Huffington Post*, October 31, 2013; www.huffingtonpost .com/john-w-pilley/animal-intelligence-descartes_b_4181893.

PLoS Biology. "Do Animals Think Like Autistic Savants?" *ScienceDaily*, February 20, 2008.

Pliny the Elder. *The Natural History of Pliny*. Vol. 2. Translated by John Bostock and H. T. Riley. London: George Bell and Sons, 1890.

Plotnik, Joshua M., Frans B. M. De Waal, and Diana Reiss. "Self-Recognition in an Asian Elephant." *Proceedings of the National Academy of Sciences* 103, no. 45 (2006): 17053–57.

Prigg, Mark. "Apes Are Sore Losers: Chimps and Bonobos Throw 'Angry Tantrums' if Taking a Risk Doesn't Pay Off." *Daily Mail*, May 29, 2013; www.dailymail.co.uk/sciencetech/article-2332837/ angry-apes-sore-losers-chimps.

Prior, Helmut, Ariane Schwarz, and Onur Gunturkun. "Mirror-Induced Behavior in the Magpie (Pica Pica): Evidence of Self-Recognition." *PLoS Biology*, August 19, 2008.

Quammen, David. "Jane: Fifty Years at Gombe." *National Geographic*, October 2010, 110–29.

Range, F., et al. "The Absence of Reward Induces Inequity Aversion in Dogs." *Proceedings of the National Academy of Sciences* 106, no. 1 (2009): 340–45.

Reiss, Diana. *The Dolphin in the Mirror: Exploring Dolphin Minds and Saving Dolphin Lives*. Boston: Houghton Mifflin Harcourt, 2011.

Romanes, George J. *Animal Intelligence*. Second ed. London: Kegan Paul, Trench, & Co., 1882; darwin-online.org.uk/content/frameset?itemID=F 1416&viewtype=text&pageseq=1.

Rosati, A. G., and B. Hare. "Chimpanzees and Bonobos Exhibit Emotional Reactions to Decision Outcomes." *PLoS ONE* 8 (2013).

Safina, Carl. *Beyond Words: What Animals Think and Feel*. New York: Henry Holt, 2015.

———. "Big Love: The Emotional Lives of Elephants." *Orion Magazine*, May/June 2015, 42–51.

Sanders, Laura. "Dog Brain Areas Respond to Voices." *Science News*, March 22, 2014, 10–11.

Santos, L. R., and A. G. Rosati. "The Evolutionary Roots of Human Decision-Making." *Annual Review of Psychology* 66 (2015): 321–47.

Scarf, Damian, Christopher Smith, and Michael Stuart. "A Spoon Full of Studies Helps the Comparison Go Down: A Comparative Analysis of

Tulving's Spoon Test." *Frontiers in Psychology* 5 (2014); www.ncbi.nlm
.nih.gov/pmc/articles/PMC4130454.

Seeley, Thomas. *Honeybee Democracy*. Princeton, N.J.: Princeton University
Press, 2010.

Shettleworth, Sara. "Animal Cognition and Animal Behavior." *Animal
Behavior* 61 (2001): 277–86.

Spinner, Stephanie. *Alex the Parrot: No Ordinary Bird*. New York: Random
House/Knopf, 2012.

Springer. "Great Apes Know They Could Be Wrong, Research Suggests."
ScienceDaily, March 23, 2010. Web, April 13, 2014; www.springer.com/
about+springer/media/springer+select?SGWID=0-11001-6-878721-0.

———. "Great Apes Think Ahead: Conclusive Evidence of Advanced
Planning Capacities." *ScienceDaily*, June 19, 2008; www.sciencedaily
.com/releases/2008/06/080618114602.htm.

Starr, Alexandra. "SeaWorld to Change Its Criticized Orca Show After Next
Year." *Two-Way*, National Public Radio, November 9, 2015; www.npr.
org/sections/thetwo-way/2015/11/09/455350162/seaworld-to-change
-its-criticized-orca-show-after-next-year.

Tan, Jingzhi, and Brian Hare. "Bonobos Share with Strangers." *PLoS One*,
January 2, 2013; journals.plos.org/plosone/article?id=10.1371/journal
.pone.0051922.

Taylor, A. H., et al. "Spontaneous Metatool Use by New Caledonian Crows."
Current Biology 17 (2007): 1504–7.

Thom, James, Nicola Clayton, and Jon Simons. "Imagining the Future—A Bird's Eye View." *The Psychologist* 26 (2013): 418–21.

Twain, Mark. *What Is Man*. Vol. 12 of *The Complete Works of Mark Twain*. New York: Harper and Brothers, 1917.

Tulving, E. "Episodic Memory and Autonoesis: Uniquely Human?" In *The Missing Link in Cognition*. New York: Oxford University Press, 2004, 4–56.

State University of New York at Buffalo. "Evidence Points to Conscious 'Metacognition' in Some Nonhuman Animals." *ScienceDaily*, September 15, 2009.

von Uexküll, Jakob. "A Stroll Through the Worlds of Animals and Men: A Picture Book of Invisible Worlds." In *Instinctive Behavior*. Translated and edited by Claire Schiller. New York: International Universities Press, 1957.

Wasserman, Edward, and Thomas Zentall. *Comparative Cognition*. Oxford: Oxford University Press, 2009.

"What Are Animals Thinking?" *NOVA*, PBS, November 7, 2012.

Wobber, V., et al. "Differences in the Early Cognitive Development of Children and Great Apes." *Developmental Psychobiology* 56, no. 3 (April 2014): 547–73.

Wynne, Clive D. L., and Monique A. R. Udell. *Animal Cognition: Evolution, Behavior and Cognition*. Basingstoke, U.K.: Palgrave Macmillan, 2013.

INDEX